REVISED COMMON LECTIONARY

Prayers

Proposed by the

Consultation on Common Texts

Fortress Press

Minneapolis

Revised Common Lectionary Prayers
Proposed by the Consultation on Common Texts

Book design: The Kantor Group, Inc.; Martin Seltz, Becky Lowe

The paper used in this publication meets the minimum requirements of American National Standard for Information Sciences—Permanence of Paper for Printed Materials, ANSI Z329.28-1984.

Manufactured in the U.S.A.

ISBN 0-8006-3484-5
07 06 05 04 03 02   1 2 3 4 5 6 7 8 9 10

CONTENTS

The proper numbers in brackets indicate the numbering system of the Roman Catholic Church and The Anglican Church of Canada.

Holy Week–Three Days

Season of Easter

Season after Pentecost (Ordinary Time)

Special Days

Writers of the Prayers 230

Index

Questionnaire 249

PREFACE

Consultation on Common Texts

The Consultation on Common Texts (CCT) originated in the mid-1960s as a forum for consultation on worship renewal among many of the major Christian churches in the United States and Canada. At the time of the development of *Revised Common Lectionary Prayers,* participants in the CCT include persons from the following churches or church agencies: American Baptist Fellowship for Liturgical Renewal, The Anglican Church of Canada, Christian Church (Disciples of Christ), Christian Reformed Church in North America, Church of the Brethren, The Episcopal Church, Evangelical Lutheran Church in America, Evangelical Lutheran Church in Canada, Free Methodist Church in Canada, International Commission on English in the Liturgy (an agency of twenty-six Roman Catholic national or international conferences of bishops), The Lutheran Church—Missouri Synod, Mennonite Church, Polish National Catholic Church of America, Presbyterian Church (U.S.A.), The Presbyterian Church in Canada, Reformed Church in America, Roman Catholic Church in the United States, Roman Catholic Church in Canada, The Unitarian Universalist Christian Fellowship, The United Church of Canada, United Church of Christ, and The United Methodist Church.

Projects and publications sponsored by the Consultation have included the following:

Revised Common Lectionary. In order to achieve even greater unity in worship, the CCT proposed a Common Lectionary as a harmonization of denominational variants in the lectionary for the Sundays and major feast days of the Christian year, based on the three-year lectionary system of the Roman Lectionary. The Common Lectionary has been revised by the Consultation on Common Texts, together with representatives of ELLC. This work has appeared under the title *The Revised Common Lectionary* (Nashville: Abingdon Press, 1992). The table of readings, reviewed for accuracy, appears also in the present volume.

Prayers We Have in Common. This project sought to provide a contemporary and ecumenical English version of prayers for the English-speaking churches around the world. Begun by the CCT, this became part of the work of the International Consultation on English Texts (ICET). These texts have now been revised by ICET's successor, the English Language Liturgical Consultation (ELLC), and published under the title *Praying Together* (Nashville: Abingdon Press, 1988). The CCT continues to work with ELLC at the international level.

A Christian Celebration of Marriage. An ecumenical liturgy for marriage was developed in response to the increasing frequency of marriage services in which more than one Christian tradition is represented. Originally published in 1985, a revised and updated version was published by Augsburg Fortress in 1995.

A Celebration of Baptism. An ecumenical liturgy for Holy Baptism was developed as a further step in the contemporary and theological convergence regarding baptism. The rite serves as an invitation to the churches to consider as official denominational rites are prepared, and it is offered for possible use in the instance of baptism when more than one Christian tradition is represented. It was published by Abingdon Press in 1988.

Earlier projects of the CCT have included *Ecumenical Services of Prayer* (1983), and *A Liturgical Psalter for the Christian Year,* prepared and edited by Massey H. Shepherd Jr., with the assistance of the CCT (1976). Current projects of the CCT include the development of a daily lectionary related to the Revised Common Lectionary.

The contents of this volume, *Revised Common Lectionary Prayers,* are more fully described in the introduction that follows. These prayers are proposed by the Consultation on Common Texts for trial use, study, and response among the churches. The questionnaire on pp. 249–256 is for the use of congregations and individuals that wish to participate in this evaluation.

Development of *Revised Common Lectionary Prayers*

The proposal for a set of ecumenical prayers specifically designed for use with the calendar of readings contained in the Revised Common Lectionary was first offered at the April 1994 meeting of the Consultation on Common Texts. At that time, several church bodies participating in the Consultation, namely, the Polish National Catholic Church of America, the Presbyterian Church (U.S.A.), and The United Methodist Church (U.S.A.), had already produced prayers, intended for use by their congregations, for one or more of the years of the Revised Common Lectionary (RCL). The International Commission on English in the Liturgy was also at work on new opening prayers for the second edition of the Roman Catholic *Lectionary for Mass,* which was the basis for the Common Lectionary both in its original and revised forms. Independent authors had also created prayers for use with the Revised Common Lectionary. However, there was no single corpus of prayers related to the readings of the RCL that intentionally sought to represent the full spectrum of Christian tradition in all its diverse richness.

A committee was appointed to look at extant texts and charged with suggesting a process by which the CCT could produce a truly ecumenical collection of prayers. The committee spent the next twenty-eight months undertaking two pieces of research. The first involved a survey of the CCT members to determine how and where each church or association used collects within the liturgy. The second involved examining several sets of prayers, both published and unpublished. The committee returned to the Consultation meeting in December of 1996 and April of 1997 with reports on the use of collects by member bodies and with a proposal for a set of ecumenical prayers.

The parameters of the project were determined largely by the results of the survey the committee had conducted. In most of these churches the prayers took the form of what has traditionally been called a *collect.*[1] Although the Sunday liturgy varied greatly in structure and content among the member bodies of the Consultation, the survey revealed that the use of the collect form of prayer by various churches fell into one of three general places within the liturgy. The actual use of the collect depended upon the particular understanding of the function of a collect in that tradition. Briefly, the survey could be summarized as follows:

- The collect appeared close to the beginning of the worship service, where its purpose was *to gather* or *collect* the people of God into sacred space and time.

- The collect was used in close proximity to the readings (usually following the readings), where its purpose was *to collect* the themes of the assigned scriptures.

- The collect followed the intercessions, where its purpose was *to collect* the multiple threads of the intercessory prayers (also called the prayers of the people or the prayers of the church) into a whole.

It became clear to the committee and to the CCT as a whole that a single collect for each Sunday could not possibly meet such diverse requirements. Therefore, it was decided to begin work on a proposal that provided three prayers for each Sunday: one intended as a gathering prayer, one intended to reflect the themes of the assigned scripture readings, and one to conclude the prayers of intercession. It was further proposed that writers be invited to compose new prayers specifically written as an offering to the ecumenical dialogue and as new ecumenical texts. Each member body of the CCT was asked to submit the names of possible writers for the project. A chairperson was appointed whose initial task was to approach potential writers and request their participation in the project.

This project was also supported by those member bodies of the CCT in which the collect as a prayer form was either not familiar or in which it ran counter to a more spontaneous tradition of prayer. These bodies included the American Baptist churches (U.S.A.), the Mennonite Church (U.S.A.), the Unitarian Universalist Christian Fellowship, and the United Church of Christ (U.S.A.).

With the approval of the CCT, the chairperson solicited input from fifteen writers, twelve of whom agreed to participate in the initial year of the project. During the twenty-six months of writing for the full three-year cycle, eleven more writers were added, bringing the total to twenty-three. There were twelve male and eleven female writers. The group consisted of both lay and ordained persons; those who were ordained included pastors in congregations, academics, and clergy employed at the denominational level. Writers represent The Anglican Church of Canada, The Episcopal Church (U.S.A.), the Evangelical Lutheran Church in Canada, the Mennonite Church (U.S.A.), The Presbyterian Church in Canada, the Roman Catholic Church (both in Canada and in the U.S.A.), the Unitarian Universalist Christian Fellowship, The United Church of Canada, the United Church of Christ (U.S.A.), and The United Methodist Church (U.S.A.). Prayers were assigned on a random basis rather than in blocks, so that the variety of voices and styles of writing would interweave across seasons and across liturgical years.

At the December 1998 meeting of CCT, a sample proposal of prayers for year C was submitted for approval, and the CCT voted to move ahead with the project and to fund the necessary meetings of an editorial board. The board was appointed, consisting of the chairperson and four additional members: the Rev. Andrea La Sonde Anastos (Unitarian Universalist Christian Fellowship), chair; the Rev. Msgr. Alan F. Detscher (Roman Catholic Church, U.S.A.), the Rev. Kevin Flynn (Anglican Church, Canada), the Rev. Judee Archer Green (Presbyterian Church, Canada), and the Rev. Clayton L. Morris (Episcopal Church, U.S.A.). At this time, a publisher was also discussed. In May of 1999, the CCT voted to pursue a publishing relationship with Augsburg Fortress, Publishers, and in late 2001 this relationship took effect.

As the project took shape, certain decisions were taken by the editorial board and endorsed by the entire Consultation. Several of these decisions concerned the content and format of the three types of collects and covered the following issues, among others.

1. Collects intended to gather the people for the beginning of the worship service were given a thematic or seasonal tone that depended less on the specific images of the readings for a particular year and more on the traditional themes of the liturgical season. One such prayer, to be used across the three-year cycle, was provided for many Sundays. These collects tend to rely strongly on imagery from the gospel readings in order to accommodate those denominations and communions in which the gospel sets the theme for preaching.

It became clear, however, that during certain times of the church year, notably the season following Epiphany and the long season after Pentecost, a different thematic or seasonal gathering prayer for every Sunday might not be necessary. The current proposal suggests that a limited number of opening prayers for those seasons, which can be used at the discretion of the worship leader, is sufficient for the Sundays in ordinary time.

2. Collects intended to work in conjunction with the intercessory prayers were submitted in several different formats. After discussion and some sampling of the different styles in worship services, the editorial board settled on a single format that provided a frame—both introduction and conclusion—for the spoken or silent intercessions of the congregation.

It was hoped that such a choice would allow for maximum flexibility, so that some communions, associations, or denominations could use both parts of the prayer as it is printed and invite intercessions in the space provided between the parts; other churches could use either portion of the prayer. This format also allows for the further option of using the introduction presented here with a traditional closing that is already familiar to the worshiping body, or a traditional opening with the closing presented here.

3. Collects intended for use in proximity to the readings were keyed to the four assigned RCL passages: the three readings and the psalm response to the first reading. Here, the broadest range of imagery was encouraged, with the particular intention of providing prayers for those churches in which the Hebrew scriptures or the second reading frequently determine the theme of worship. Collects in this set often use images and addresses from Hebrew scriptures, including the psalm assigned for the day.

In the season after Pentecost, where the RCL provides two tracks of readings, the editorial board attempted to provide a sizeable number of collects that emphasize the themes of the semicontinuous readings. These prayers seek to honor the internal integrity of the Hebrew scriptures and are thus theocentric rather than christocentric.

The editorial board met four times for two or more days at each meeting, between August 1998 and August 2000. All prayers were received by the chairperson and submitted to the board without name or denominational affiliation attached. Editors were assigned seasonal blocks of material so that, over the course of the three-year cycle, each member of the board did initial editing on the work of every writer, and each editor worked with three different seasonal blocks of material. Initial editing suggestions for each prayer were compiled into a document and presented to the entire board, with the board completing the editing as a committee of the whole. The material for each liturgical year was submitted, in its entirety, to the whole CCT for written comments. Comments from the CCT were then brought back to the editorial board and further work was done on every prayer.

As the board began to work, several theological and practical issues emerged. The theological issues elicited profoundly challenging discussions, both within the board and at full meetings of the CCT; these issues are covered more fully later in this introduction in the section on theological considerations.

The practical issues proved to be equally complex and involved some expansion and reshaping of the project itself. Early in the writing process, as mentioned previously, it was agreed that during the season after Pentecost, when the RCL offers two tracks of readings from the Hebrew scriptures (a semicontinuous track and a thematic track), two collects would be needed for each Sunday to meet the requirements of those denominations, communions, and associations that use the prayer to collect the themes of the readings.

As the project neared completion, however, the editorial board realized that the collects intended for the *beginning* of the worship service as gathering prayers for the post-Pentecost season were almost exclusively gospel-centered, often with no clear reference to themes of the first reading or psalm. It became apparent that the project had not successfully provided useful prayers for those churches in which preaching on the Hebrew scriptures was a strong tradition that influenced a particular service. These churches used the collect not in conjunction with the readings, but as the prayer to gather the people of God. A set of thematic collects based on the semicontinuous readings from the Hebrew scriptures was added; these collects were intended for use over two or more appropriate Sundays during the season after Pentecost.

A more critical issue arose in August 1998. It became clear to the editorial board during its work that the ending sentences of approximately half of the prayers—in some cases doxologies, and in other cases, other theological formulas—presented a potential problem. The intent of the project was to make available an *ecumenical* corpus of collects. From the beginning it was understood that not every prayer in the document would be equally useful for every denomination or communion; however, it was hoped that an overlapping majority of the prayers would be appropriate for every one of the member bodies. For some member churches, a concluding formula was essential for theological reasons and left little room for flexibility in its formula (doxological or nondoxological). For other member churches, the concluding formula provided a keying phrase that would alert the congregation to prepare for the corporate "Amen." Again, these phrases were traditional and did not permit much alteration or they became confusing and no longer fulfilled their purpose. For a third group of churches, concluding doxologies or formulas were unfamiliar and the preference was for prayers that ended with a simple "Amen."

A compromise position was reached by the Consultation: all collects intended for the opening *(collecting)* position in the worship service would be given such an ending except those specifically written to highlight the semicontinuous Hebrew scripture readings in the post-Pentecost season. Those collects intended for use with the prayers of the people would be given such endings as often as possible. Those collects used in conjunction with the readings would be given such endings only where the style of the prayer made it appropriate. The CCT affirmed that the use of the collects in individual congregations would, within the parameters of each church body's requirements, be at the discretion of the clergy and worship leaders of that congregation. Therefore, concluding words might be deleted where they are present or added where they do not exist in the printed prayer in order to reflect the needs of particular contexts.

At the August 2000 meeting of the editorial board, the final work was done to create a document totaling 375 new ecumenical collects. The board submitted this final draft to the entire CCT in December 2000 and the manuscript was approved for publication as a proposal to the churches, with feedback requested for use in a potential future revision.

Purpose

From its inception in the mid-1960s, the work of the Consultation on Common Texts has been shaped and motivated by a three-fold purpose: to "prepar[e] liturgical texts and documents, as a forum for the exchange of information regarding the development of liturgy among . . . Churches, [and] . . . to engage in tasks related to liturgy on an ecumenical basis."[2] The most extensive piece of work undertaken by the CCT to date was the fifteen years of labor that began in 1978, produced the Common Lectionary in 1983, and issued the Revised Common Lectionary (RCL) in 1992. The steady acceptance of the RCL in ecumenical as well as denominational settings, not only within North America, but around the world, led quite naturally to a discussion of how and whether the CCT would choose to support that document with further materials.

The idea of a cycle of prayers keyed to the lectionary was raised from time to time in CCT meetings both prior to the lectionary's revision and then, with increasing frequency, following the publication of the RCL. Specific requests for such prayers began to surface both from members of the English Language Liturgical Commission

(ELLC), of which CCT is a founding member, and from the member bodies of CCT. As mentioned in the previous section, these requests coalesced as a proposal in April of 1994.

The initial decision to proceed with a study of the project was made without regard for any of the potential difficulties inherent in it. Rather, it was motivated primarily by two simple questions: Was such a project feasible? and Did such a project fill a void or otherwise advance the ecumenical dialogue around liturgical texts? Once both questions were answered in the affirmative, substantive discussions began about the purpose that would drive the writing, editing, and publication.

These conversations were complex and far-ranging. The broad mandate given to the editorial board, which was intended to insure a spacious and flexible creative environment, recognized that the Consultation's best work would emerge from a deep engagement with process and with unanticipated questions arising during the completion of a specific project. In the course of this work, certain areas of consensus were reached and are briefly summarized here.

First, the Consultation enthusiastically affirmed that the resulting document must be ecumenical in the broadest way possible. That agreement led to some inescapable consequences. The final prayers would reflect many voices and many styles, some familiar to particular member bodies, and others that arose spontaneously from the invitation to engage with scripture on behalf of the *ecumenical* community. Thus, the collection, by its very nature, would begin to expand the boundaries around the issue of univocal corporate prayer.[3] It was acknowledged that the result would be a collection in which not every prayer would be equally useful to every member body or worship leader. The intent of the process was not to find a "lowest common denominator" nor to settle for a bland uniformity, but to spark profound dialogue and to work in a catalytic fashion within the broad ecumenical community.

Second, the Consultation affirmed that the proposed prayers would be based on and complementary to the readings assigned by the Revised Common Lectionary. Some liturgical texts tend to highlight differences among the churches because their purpose is to teach or confirm doctrinal identity. By asking writers to ground the collects in commonly held scripture, it was hoped that the project would produce material that served to unite rather than divide.

Third, the Consultation recognized that the ecumenical nature of the project would result in a proposal that would nudge every reader and every one of the member bodies beyond a personal or corporate "comfort zone."

Finally, the Consultation reiterated its foundational commitment to dialogue and mutual nurture. Although the CCT naturally expected excellence in the quality of the prayers, it was never expected that this collection would stand for all time as the definitive corpus of ecumenical collects. The document that follows is only a first and, in some ways, risky step:

- seeking to offer examples of corporate prayer that are both multivocal and respectful of the variety of traditions from which they arise;

- intended to provide resources for personal, corporate, and ecumenical prayer and to provide material for study and discussion both within and between churches;

- designed to prove useful to covenanted or communal bodies, whether associations of churches or communions, but also designed for use by individual members of the clergy and lay worship leaders.

Stylistic Considerations

Because previous Consultation projects involving texts had always begun with material *already* held in common by the member bodies and moved outward slowly and deliberately from that core commonality, we were not fully prepared for the consequences of working from a place of challenging diversity *toward* commonality. This aspect, however, proved to be the richest part of the experience.

The first intense and lively discussions were held by the editorial board when it read the initial set of 112 collects. One example of an unanticipated place of contention will illustrate how disconcerting the project appeared in its first months. The decision had already been made, when the initial parameters for the prayers were composed, that the final project would consist not only of collects in the traditional one-sentence format familiar from *The Book of Common Prayer*, but would also include collects in the more contemporary two-sentence format currently being used by ICEL. The board observed that this seemingly minor variation in style had enormous impact on the effect of the collect and led to prayers that were more direct and less rounded in tone. As it wrestled with this and other tensions between familiar forms and language and the striking freshness of over three-quarters of the submitted collects, the board was able to identify several key areas for further discussion.

Briefly, these observations fell under one of two large overarching topics: the use of scripture and the use of language. Obviously, the images of scripture and choice of language influence and inform one another, and an observation about one often presented implications for a discussion of the other. For the purposes of internal work as well as broad discussion among the whole CCT, however, the board attempted to clarify and separate the two topics.

Scripture and scriptural images

An exegetical and "objective" reading of the lessons on which each prayer was based revealed that scripture itself is considerably more ambiguous and multivalent than is evident from within the context of any single tradition. The editorial board noted some factors that contribute to a consistent or uniform reading of scripture within any particular tradition.

Three areas of concern emerged:

First, preaching and teaching within a specific association, communion, or denomination, almost without exception, carries the burden of conveying not only the message of scripture itself, but the doctrinal identity of the church body. Over time, this pattern leads to forming or creating a lens of consistency through which members of that church body interpret the Bible. Scripture texts that cannot be focused through this lens are frequently ignored, dismissed, or "preached over," leading to a cycle that steadily reaffirms a narrowed impression of the sacred story.

Such preaching and teaching lead quite naturally to a relatively narrow use of biblical imagery. The specific emphasis of church teaching influences, for instance, titles used for the Divine and the qualities or aspects of the Divine, which are developed in corporate prayer. Thus, church bodies that preach and teach universal salvation tend to use divine addresses that invoke redemptive love or care (e.g., Holy Shepherd, Father) and avoid addresses the invoke judgment or authority (e.g., Almighty Judge, King of Kings). Pentecostal churches tend to use Spirit imagery and address prayers to the Spirit with much more frequency than do some other church bodies. Over generations, this tendency encourages members of particular associations, denominations, or communions to feel comfortable with certain scriptural language and to be startled by less familiar images.

Furthermore, the relative validity of and relationship between First and Second Testaments for a particular church body creates a tension in how images from the Hebrew scriptures, the Apocrypha, or the deuterocanonical books are used in corporate worship. Again, the teachings of the denomination, communion, or association produce a lens that, at one extreme of the continuum, sees the Old Testament as totally separate from the New and regards it as extraneous to Christian faith or, at the other extreme, sees the use of the Hebrew scriptures in worship exclusively in a typological manner in relation to the gospel. Exactly where a church body falls along that continuum strongly influences its comfort with any prayer that is not overtly christocentric.

A second area of concern was initially articulated by the board as a *theological* issue, a more finely tuned expression of the tension between First and Second Testaments. More introspection led the board to look carefully at sets of prayers (collects, pastoral prayers, intercessory prayers, litanies) that were written and published for use within a specific tradition. This mini-study revealed that the vast majority of historical prayers and contemporary interdenominational prayers—even those that invoked scriptural images or themes—are doctrinal, didactic, or apologetic in content. When the CCT chose to invite collects that arose from and returned to scripture and intentionally avoided doctrinal or apologetic content, the issues that arose were *linguistic* as well as theological.

A third area that occasioned challenges had to do with the liturgical traditions connected to particular holy days and seasons, and with the understanding of the purpose or meaning of the various liturgical seasons within different church bodies. This issue was particularly salient where the culture has so co-opted the meaning of a church season that major reclamation is needed (as with the season of Advent for most churches) or where communions or denominations with a more complex liturgy have needs different from churches with a simpler liturgy (Ash Wednesday and the Triduum being two examples.)

It might be broadly observed that the greater the eschatological meaning of a specific holy day or season within a particular tradition, the more dissatisfaction emerged with collects reflective of scripture rather than doctrine. Such collects did not successfully convey enough of the churches' teaching about the occasion. Ecclesial traditions in which such holy days or seasons were understood more as a memorial, or were newly introduced (or re-introduced), or were left entirely to the discretion of the individual parish, were more critical of collects that seemed heavily thematic at the expense of the simple or straightforward images of scripture. The three prayers for Maundy Thursday provide the best example of successful compromise over this tension; certain prayers for Passion Sunday and for Good Friday, on the other hand, are examples of prayers that did not completely resolve these issues.

Matters of language

Three areas of linguistic usage generated considerable discussion and some discomfort in the process of developing these prayers: succinctness of style, content that includes startling images and seeks to avoid theological jargon, and the use of a personal tone within corporate prayer. Consensus was not reached within the board and the CCT that all decisions made concerning these areas of discussion satisfactorily addressed the complexity of the issues and the diversity of expectations among the member bodies. These matters require further honest and challenging conversation in ecumenical forums, and it is the CCT's hope that feedback and response to these prayers will contribute to that conversation.

First, although the collect is a notably succinct form of prayer, it is at the mercy of the parenthetical phrase and the rhythm of the English language. Writers and editors for this project tended to smooth rough edges in a given prayer by inserting filler phrases such as "we pray." Where a hitch in rhythm was not solved by a filler phrase, it was often addressed by what the board came to call "the wildly proliferating adjective." When these two tendencies were noted, filler phrases were eliminated and lists of adjectives were pared to one or two. The resulting "silences," where a familiar word or two would traditionally have been heard or where an adjectival list had kept the rhythm consistent, initially seemed awkward. It also resulted in prayers that were denser in content and that required more attentive listening.

These collects are offered with some of their rough edges still intact, avoiding extraneous words and phrases that would strip a prayer of its vitality or power. When the collects are read aloud with careful preparation and listened to with similar care, the richness of their language and content promises to outweigh the initial difficulty that may be encountered with this economic use of language.

Second, beyond the issue already mentioned concerning the unfamiliar feel of collects that were less doctrinal and more scriptural in content, the board noticed in these prayers the use of words and phrases that would be meaningless to new converts or to people who had been away from worship for an extended time. It was even suspected that although many faithful Christians might be able to define these terms, they would be limited to a rote recitation from a childhood catechism or to a recollection of a brief definition offered by a pastor in sermons or Bible study. The board called this "the jargon factor."

Although these specialized words were all legitimate theological terms[4] that carry many layers of meaning for scholars or the spiritually mature, and although they sound appropriate in prayers because they are familiar "religious words" to generations of church-goers, they often served to reduce the specificity of the collect. Where such words stood alone or as one in a list of terms rather than being developed in the body of the prayer, they were generally excised. Naturally, the identification of jargon is somewhat subjective: the process may have removed words that are more commonly and fully understood than was reflected by the collective experience of the board, and the process may have retained some words or phrases that the majority of hearers will find meaningless. This issue also calls for further dialogue concerning questions such as the following. Jesus taught in the vernacular; how does the language of worship convey the truth of faith without obscuring it? How can the church employ terms essential for communicating faith concepts without falling into exclusionary or intellectually self-serving jargon? If language about God is ultimately metaphor, how can the richness of poetic language avoid becoming so high-flown as to be meaningless? Does the current reality require the church to grapple more deeply with some of its in-house terms, redefining them for the present age?

Operating from the stance that faith is meant to be transparent rather than clouded, open rather than esoteric,[5] the editorial board decided to eliminate those words or phrases, primarily doctrinal terms, that tended to confuse or complicate the prayers. It was also observed that the use of such words and phrases has frequently created conflict between communions, associations, and denominations because they have often marked the boundaries that differentiate one Christian tradition from another.

A related concern regarding content the board termed "the startle factor." As writers worked more deeply with scripture, jarring and abrasive images began to appear in prayers. When the use of these images was questioned, a reexamination of the readings typically revealed that the image was present in the text. The editorial board eventually acknowledged that prayer language has often been sanitized over many generations, and that some biblical images have been ignored or totally avoided. Thus, certain words were retained (e.g., *lust,* a word not often used in prayer), and others were eliminated for pastoral reasons (e.g., *drunk* in a Pentecost prayer). Responses to the unexpected or startling images present in these prayers are especially welcomed from those who use this resource.

Finally, the board observed that the freshness of the collects submitted for this project came, to a surprisingly large extent, from the intimate quality of the language used and from a vulnerability on the part of the writers to offer, for corporate use, their personal response to the power of a particular passage. The editorial board and the CCT wrestled deeply with the question of the extent to which language used in private or personal prayer was appropriate for corporate prayer.

It was noted that questions of corporate usefulness tended to be aroused when language was:

- simpler rather than more complex. Direct words like *money* or *greed* felt more challenging to some than more abstract terms like *sharing* or *generosity.*

- challenging to the status quo of the society or its current idols. Again, direct words around or about money, power, and accomplishment caused discomfort.

- reflective of minority experience. Words or images about female experience of birth or nurture raised the question, "But how can *men* relate to those words in corporate prayer?" Words and images that reflected the experience of those who were disenfranchised, ignored, dispossessed, or oppressed felt "alien" to the experience of privilege.

- raw, unusual, or intimate. Words such as *naked, drunk, frenzy, shame,* or *brutality* challenged former boundaries of public language, as did phrases that suggested that our grief, pain, anger, fear, or prejudice—either as people or community— were not in control (e.g., Passion Sunday, year B).

Participants in the conversation acknowledged that the evaluation of corporate usefulness often seemed to be more a matter of emotional response than being based in any objective criteria. Another point of view held that the dichotomy between public or corporate prayer and private or personal prayer was a construct reflecting a preference developed and nurtured, whether intentionally or unintentionally, by denominations, associations, or communions, rather than an objective or absolute reality. It was also acknowledged that, even though styles and choices of language may be held in a corporate memory and, therefore, validated strongly by tradition, the connection of the soul with God is an individual experience even when it is occasioned within the context of corporate liturgy. Thus, although prayer may be spoken publicly, it will resonate or fail to resonate, express or fail to express, a personal knowledge and relationship. Given the nature of communal worship, any single prayer will be univocal at the time it is prayed. In this ecumenical proposal, however, the CCT determined to make the *collection* of prayers multivocal across its breadth so that it reflected, as far as is possible at the current time, a variety of imagery, language, style, and experience.

The CCT invites the churches as well as individual readers to explore and experiment with the attempts made here to address the matter of the relationship of public and private prayer. Ecumenical dialogue and response offers an opportunity to confront places of resistance or need, of comfort or anxiety, of familiarity or new life, and to be renewed continually by the Holy Spirit.

Theological Considerations

During the course of this project, stylistic considerations that emerged concerning form and language were complemented by theological considerations. Choices of language shape and are shaped by human conceptions of the Holy One and by how the self-disclosure of God through scripture and personal revelation is understood. It is equally true that our relationship with God will influence the language and content of our prayer. Therefore, observations about style and observations about theology cannot in any real way be separated from one another. Certain theological, christological, and ecclesial doctrines, however, provided the starting point for especially fruitful conversations in which style and language could be set aside for extensive periods. The CCT identified these as fertile territory for further ecumenical dialogue, hoping that the collects themselves will serve as catalysts for such dialogue.

It is beyond the scope of this introduction to name or describe a complete list of such concepts; however, it is hoped that the following will serve as a springboard for communal study—both teaching and learning—and will serve as places of wrestling and places of blessing among Christian denominations, associations, and communions. Praying in and through such discussions, may we meet God face-to-face.

Understandings of *salvation, election, sin,* and, to a lesser degree, *reconciliation* revealed the greatest diversity among member bodies. A writer who believes in universal salvation produces prayers quite different in tone and content from one who believes in predestination or election. Understandings of sin (especially in relation to election, predestination, and salvation) were highly nuanced and included conversations about original sin; human brokenness; separation from God, other, and self; reconciliation; the Fall; the relationship between Adam and Jesus; the consonance-dissonance between Eve and Mary; eternal damnation; and psycho-theological ideas of integration. [See the following prayers: Palm Sunday (scripture, year A), Holy Week (fourth thematic prayer) Maundy Thursday (intercessory), Proper 13 (scripture, year B, series 1), and Proper 24 (scripture, year C, series 1) for a selection representing different concepts of salvation.]

Concepts of *justice* and *equity* led to discussions that branched in two different directions. One branch addressed justice and equity in relation to *mercy*. These discussions invariably included overtones of sin and salvation, especially as the discussion moved toward mercy among and between persons, forgiveness and reconciliation, and God's mercy toward creation. The other branch sought an understanding of justice and equity in relation to the gospel mandate that arises from the prophecy in Hebrew scripture. An example of the latter branch is found in the thematic prayer for Ash Wednesday.

Various theologies of *ecology, environment,* and *stewardship* (trusteeship) also invited two very different discussions. The first included *creationism* and *evolution, domination* and *interdependence,* and humanity's relative importance within or authority over creation. The second discussion tended to highlight concepts of the *immanence* and *transcendence* of God, and to wrestle with panentheism and other expressions of a living earth.

A highly sensitive area of discussion concerned *grace* and *works.* The majority of the writers for this project tended to move the focus of the collects beyond *praying* for others towards *acting* on behalf of others. Within the Consultation, however, greater diversity of opinion emerged about this area. For some, the use of action verbs such as *work, serve, act, contend,* and even *proclaim* raised concerns about pelagianism or semi-pelagianism. The diversity of opinion on this matter reveals the continuing challenge and opportunity for ecumenical dialogue regarding the relationship of grace and works, which for some seem to exist as two ends of a continuum and for others as a dynamic whole, grace inspiring works and works, in turn, deepening an awareness of grace.

Christology, "high," "low," and everywhere between provoked intense dialogue and, in this area, language was particularly important. Language expressing the humanity and divinity of Jesus the Christ carried enormous theological and emotional weight. [See the second scripture prayer for Christmas, proper II, and the scripture prayer for Christmas, proper III, for examples of two very different christologies.]

The conversation revealed that creedal and non-creedal churches need to be particularly careful in defining and using terms with one another. It was also observed that the understanding of the relationship among the three persons of the Trinity is far more diverse than might have been expected. Lively conversations about an "economic" versus a "relational" Trinity (especially involving the work of Catherine LaCugna) raised issues of language and the relative expansiveness or narrowness of acceptable trinitarian language in corporate and private prayer.

The vision of God's *reign, realm, kingdom, country,* and *commonwealth* brought conversations back to *salvation* and *election,* as well as touching on *justice* and *mercy,* and relative understandings of human *domination over* or *interdependence with* the rest of creation. Preferences about language used to describe that which follows the parousia also generated discussion, much of it focused on the words used to describe the temporal political reality in which we live or have lived. Two collects, both assigned for All Saints, depict this eternal hope in different ways. [See the thematic prayer and the year C scripture prayer for that day.]

A related discussion involved the concepts of *now* versus *not yet*. [See Lent 2. The intercessory collect tends toward one end of that continuum and the scripture collect for year C tends toward the other end.] The tension between *now* and *not yet*, however, also has enormous impact on discussions of *justice* and *equity*, and *stewardship of creation*.

Conclusion

It is with profound hope that the Consultation on Common Texts commends this work to the ecumenical community. We commend it to you enthusiastically, recognizing that not every prayer will be useful for every gathered community of faith. And we commend it to you acknowledging that our consensus to propose this collection of prayers for study and response does not mean that every word garnered the full approval of each member body, but that we endorse the direction and intention of the project and believe that it contains material to enrich and nurture every denomination, communion, or association. We are deeply desirous to hear from those who use these materials in public worship via the questionnaire at the end of this volume or through other appropriate means.

We believe that these prayers raise some essential liturgical and theological issues for the Christian community, and open areas of dialogue where the churches have not engaged fully with one another in the past, but may productively do so in the future. We sought to be faithful both to our purpose as a Consultation and to our calling as individual Christians.

We express our profound gratitude to the women and men willing to step into new territory with these collects and to offer them generously for the good of the whole body of Christ. Their work reflects the renewing current of abundant life always flowing within the wide and widely diverse community of those who are disciples of Jesus of Nazareth, the one we confess as Christ.

May the Spirit, praying through these prayers, bless you, whether you are alone or in communion with others when you pray them.

Andrea La Sonde Anastos
Chairperson, CCT Collects Editorial Board
The Epiphany of the Lord, 2002

Footnotes

1. The term *collect* comes from the reference in Western liturgies to *collectio, collecta,* or *ad collectam,* literally "assembly." *The New Westminster Dictionary of Liturgy and Worship* describes the form of the prayer as follows:

    Ancient examples of the collect after the entrance, of which many survive to this day in the Roman rite, exhibit an all but unvarying structure: 1. an address to God . . .; 2. a reference to some divine attribute or act as a ground for prayer; 3. the prayer proper, short, simple and definite; 4. a concluding doxology, offering the prayer to the Father through the Son and in the Holy Spirit.*

    In *The Book of Common Prayer,* the collect invariably appears in a single sentence format with a colon (:) serving to separate parts one and two from parts three and four. More recent collects (e.g., the collects prepared by the International Commission on the Liturgy) have replaced the colon with a period, resulting in a two-sentence format that is more in keeping with modern rules of punctuation. Revised Common Lectionary *Prayers* occasionally uses a three-sentence format in order to avoid the overuse of the semicolon (;), which has a tendency to trip up the reader.

2. "The Purpose of the Consultation on Common Texts" in *Guidelines and Procedures,* approved April 1996 by the CCT.

3. Most corporate prayer is, by its nature, univocal in its presentation of petitions, praise, and intercessions on behalf of the whole gathered people, whether the words apply to them or not. It can be problematic when a prayer is presented to be read in unison by the assembly, which may force an individual to speak words he or she cannot affirm or to remain silent.

    These prayers attempt to address this concern by providing a wide variety of images, styles, tones, and themes reflective of a broad range of experiences. A conscious effort has been made to eliminate language that excludes whole groups of people by the use of language that, in the past, has been hurtful to persons by demeaning or invalidating their experience or by equating physical, mental, or emotional traits with goodness or evilness of soul.

4. Among other terms, the editorial board found it needed to be cautious about words such as *righteousness, humility, glory, covenant, discipleship,* and *salvation* where they stood alone and their theological freight or content was not more fully developed in the collect. A different problem arose with *word [Word],* which, when *heard* rather than *read,* was occasionally confusing. Finally, some phrases sounded reasonable until the question was asked, "What meaning does this convey to the average worshiper? to a convert? to a seeker?" Examples of such phrases include the following: "according to your purpose [or promise] in Christ Jesus," "your Spirit of revelation," "the way of the cross," "that our confession be praise," and "through [Christ] reach completion."

5. See, for instance, Matthew 10:26-27; Luke 12:2-3; John 18:19-21.

*Davies, J.G. ed. *The New Westminster Dictionary of Liturgy and Worship.* Philadelphia: The Westminster Press, 1986.

Note on the Conclusions of the Prayers

The majority of the prayers in this collection have formal conclusions incorporated into them that are either doxological or christological. These conclusions are not intended to be prescriptive. As stated earlier in the introduction, those churches or associations that do not normally use a concluding phrase or doxology should feel free to omit them. Equally, if the conclusion given in a specific prayer is not in keeping with a particular liturgical tradition, it may be rewritten or replaced with a conclusion customary to that church.

Some prayers do not have any conclusion or ending. This practice is likewise not intended to be prescriptive. Within those traditions that prefer or require such a conclusion, it may be added by the worship planner or the person leading the prayer in worship. Longer or shorter conclusions customary in a particular tradition may be used. The following examples are also offered as alternative endings.

Traditional Conclusions

Long Conclusions

When the prayer is addressed to the first person of the Trinity:
We ask this [*or* We pray] through our Lord Jesus Christ, your Son,
who lives and reigns with you and the Holy Spirit, one God,
for ever and ever [*or* now and for ever].

When the prayer is addressed to Christ or mentions Christ at the end:
You live and reign with the Father and the Holy Spirit, one God,
for ever and ever [*or* now and for ever].

or
. . . who lives and reigns with the Father and the Holy Spirit, one God,
for ever and ever [*or* now and for ever].

When the prayer is addressed to the Holy Spirit or mentions the Spirit at the end:
You live and reign with the Father and the Son, one God,
for ever and ever [*or* now and for ever].

or
. . . who lives and reigns with the Father and the Son, one God,
for ever and ever [*or* now and for ever].

Short Conclusions

When the prayer is addressed to the first person of the Trinity:
We ask this [*or* Grant this *or* We pray] through Christ our Lord [*or* Savior].

When the prayer is addressed to Christ or mentions Christ at the end:
We ask this [*or* Grant this *or* We pray] through Christ our Lord [*or* Savior].

or
. . . who is Lord for ever and ever [*or* now and for ever].

or
. . . who lives and reigns for ever and ever [*or* now and for ever].

When the prayer is addressed to the Spirit:
We ask this [*or* Grant this *or* We pray] through the same Holy Spirit,
for ever and ever [*or* now and for ever].

or
. . . who is Lord forever and ever [*or* now and for ever].

Nontraditional Conclusions

Even though certain conclusions may have the weight of theological tradition behind them or serve a practical purpose such as a keying phrase for a communal "Amen," new or less traditional endings may be in keeping with the theme or imagery of the prayer, particularly with scripture prayers that reflect the readings from Hebrew scripture.

The following endings are examples that might be useful for those church bodies in which the worship often centers around the first reading or the psalm.

. . . for you are [*or* . . . to you who are] our Creator, our Redeemer, our Sustainer,
     now and always.

. . . for we entrust ourselves to you who create, redeem, and sustain us,
     now and in the time to come.

. . . for you are always worthy of our praise and thanksgiving.

. . . that [through these actions] we may honor you who bless us abundantly.

. . . that we may manifest your presence with us [*or* in the world].

. . . that through your grace the world may be created anew.

We ask this of you who are our Peace, our Truth, our Way.

We ask this through the Spirit who is our Guide and Advocate.

Advent

First Sunday of Advent

Thematic

God of justice and peace,
from the heavens you rain down mercy and kindness,
that all on earth may stand in awe and wonder
before your marvelous deeds.
Raise our heads in expectation,
that we may yearn for the coming day of the Lord
and stand without blame before your Son, Jesus Christ,
who lives and reigns for ever and ever. Amen.

Intercessory

We seek the mighty God
in the most unlikely places
as a child in a stable,
and in an empty tomb.
May God hear these prayers,
which come from the unlikely corners of our lives.

Prayers of the People, concluding with:

Give us ears to hear, O God,
and eyes to watch,
that we may know your presence in our midst
during this holy season of joy
as we anticipate the coming of Jesus Christ. Amen.

Scripture

YEAR A
Isaiah 2:1-5
Psalm 122
Romans 13:11-14
Matthew 24:36-44

Unexpected God,
your advent alarms us.
Wake us from drowsy worship,
from the sleep that neglects love,
and the sedative of misdirected frenzy.
Awaken us now to your coming,
and bend our angers into your peace. Amen.

YEAR B
Isaiah 64:1-9
Psalm 80:1-7, 17-19
1 Corinthians 1:3-9
Mark 13:24-37

Creator of the world,
you are the potter, we are the clay,
and you form us in your image.
Shape our spirits
by Christ's transforming power,
that as one people
we may live out your compassion and justice,
whole and sound in the realm of your peace. Amen.

YEAR C
Jeremiah 33:14-16
Psalm 25:1-10
1 Thessalonians 3:9-13
Luke 21:25-36

O God of all the prophets,
you herald the coming of the Son of Man
by wondrous signs in the heavens and on the earth.
Guard our hearts from despair so that we,
in the company of the faithful
and by the power of your Holy Spirit,
may be found ready to raise our heads
at the coming near of our redemption,
the day of Jesus Christ. Amen.

Second Sunday of Advent

Thematic

God of timeless grace,
you fill us with joyful expectation.
Make us ready for the message that prepares the way,
that with uprightness of heart and holy joy
we may eagerly await the kingdom of your Son, Jesus Christ,
who reigns with you and the Holy Spirit, now and for ever. Amen.

Intercessory

God of hope,
you raised up John the baptizer
as a herald who calls us to conversion.
As we joyfully await the glorious coming of Christ,
we pray to you for the needs of the church and the world.

Prayers of the People, concluding with:

Hear our humble prayer
that we may serve you in holiness and faith
and give voice to your presence among us
until the day of the coming of your Son, Jesus Christ,
who lives and reigns for ever and ever. Amen.

Scripture

YEAR A
Isaiah 11:1-10
Psalm 72:1-7, 18-19
Romans 15:4-13
Matthew 3:1-12

Laboring God,
with axe and winnowing fork
you clear a holy space
where hurt and destruction have no place,
and a little child holds sway.
Clear our lives of hatred and despair,
sow seeds of joy and peace,
that shoots of hope may spring forth
and we may live in harmony
with one another. Amen.

YEAR B
Isaiah 40:1-11
Psalm 85:1-2, 8-13
2 Peter 3:8-15a
Mark 1:1-8

God of hope,
you call us from the exile of our sin
with the good news of restoration;
you build a highway through the wilderness;
you come to us and bring us home.
Comfort us with the expectation of your saving power,
made known to us in Jesus Christ our Lord. Amen.

YEAR C
Baruch 5:1-9 *or* Malachi 3:1-4
Luke 1:68-79
Philippians 1:3-11
Luke 3:1-6

Out of the embrace of mercy and righteousness,
you have brought forth joy and dignity for your people,
O Holy One of Israel.
Remember now your ancient promise:
make straight the paths that lead to you,
and smooth the rough ways,
that in our day
we might bring forth your compassion
for all humanity. Amen.

Third Sunday of Advent

Thematic

God of hope,
you call us home from the exile of selfish oppression
to the freedom of justice,
the balm of healing,
and the joy of sharing.
Make us strong to join you in your holy work,
as friends of strangers and victims,
companions of those whom others shun,
and as the happiness of those whose hearts are broken.
We make our prayer through Jesus Christ our Lord.
Amen.

Intercessory

Brothers and sisters,
as we joyfully await the glorious coming of the Christ,
let us pray for the needs of the church, our community, and the world.

Prayers of the People, concluding with:

God of joy and exultation,
you strengthen what is weak;
you enrich the poor
and give hope to those who live in fear.
Look upon our needs this day.
Make us grateful for the good news of salvation
and keep us faithful in your service
until the coming of our Lord Jesus Christ,
who lives for ever and ever. Amen.

Scripture

YEAR A
Isaiah 35:1-10
Psalm 146:5-10 *or* Luke 1:47-55
James 5:7-10
Matthew 11:2-11

O God of Isaiah and John the Baptist,
through all such faithful ones
you proclaim the unfolding of future joy
and renewed life.
Strengthen our hearts to believe your advent promise
that one day we will walk in the holy way of Christ,
where sorrow and sighing will be no more
and the journey of God's people will be joy. Amen.

YEAR B
Isaiah 61:1-4, 8-11
Psalm 126 *or* Luke 1:47-55
1 Thessalonians 5:16-24
John 1:6-8, 19-28

Merciful God of peace,
your word, spoken by the prophets,
restores your people's life and hope.
Fill our hearts with the joy of your saving grace,
that we may hold fast to your great goodness
and in our lives proclaim your justice in all the world. Amen.

YEAR C
Zephaniah 3:14-20
Isaiah 12:2-6
Philippians 4:4-7
Luke 3:7-18

O God of the exiles and the lost,
you promise restoration and wholeness
through the power of Jesus Christ.
Give us faith to live joyfully,
sustained by your promises
as we eagerly await the day when they will be fulfilled
for all the world to see,
through the coming of your Son, Jesus Christ. Amen.

Fourth Sunday of Advent

Thematic

O God of Elizabeth and Mary,
you visited your servants with news of the world's redemption
in the coming of the Savior.
Make our hearts leap with joy,
and fill our mouths with songs of praise,
that we may announce glad tidings of peace,
and welcome the Christ in our midst. Amen.

Intercessory

Brothers and sisters,
as we joyfully await the glorious coming of the Christ,
let us pray for the needs of the church, our community, and the world.

Prayers of the People, concluding with:

God of promise,
you have given us a sign of your love
through the gift of Jesus Christ, our Savior,
who was promised from ages past.
We believe as Joseph did
the message of your presence
whispered by an angel,
and offer our prayers for your world,
confident of your care and mercy for all creation. Amen.

Scripture

YEAR A
Isaiah 7:10-16
Psalm 80:1-7, 17-19
Romans 1:1-7
Matthew 1:18-25

Shepherd of Israel,
may Jesus, Emmanuel and son of Mary,
be more than just a dream in our hearts.
With the apostles, prophets, and saints,
save us, restore us,
and lead us in the way of grace and peace,
that we may bear your promise into the world. Amen.

YEAR B
2 Samuel 7:1-11, 16
Luke 1:47-55 *or* Psalm 89:1-4, 19-26
Romans 16:25-27
Luke 1:26-38

Ever-faithful God,
through prophets and angels
you promised to raise up a holy child
who would establish a household of peace and justice.
Open our hearts to receive your Son,
that we may open our doors
to welcome all people as sisters and brothers,
and establish your household in our time. Amen.

YEAR C
Micah 5:2-5a
Luke 1:47-55 *or* Psalm 80:1-7
Hebrews 10:5-10
Luke 1:39-45, [46-55]

O Shepherd of Israel,
you gently support the one who is with child
and call forth the Lamb who dances in the womb.
Stir our hearts to recognize Christ's coming,
as Elizabeth recognized his presence
in Mary's radiant obedience to your desire,
and open our souls to receive the one
who came to love your flock. Amen.

Christmas

Seasonal Prayers

Thematic

O Holy One,
heavenly angels spoke to earthly shepherds
and eternity entered time in the child of Bethlehem.
Through the telling of the Christmas story,
let our temporal lives be caught up in the eternal
in that same child,
that we might join shepherds and all the heavenly host
in praising the coming of Jesus Christ, our Savior. Amen.

OR

God of glory,
your splendor shines from a manger in Bethlehem,
where the Light of the world is humbly born
into the darkness of human night.
Open our eyes to Christ's presence in the shadows of our world,
so that we, like him, may become beacons of your justice,
and defenders of all for whom there is no room. Amen.

OR

Light of life, you came in flesh,
born into human pain and joy,
and gave us power to be your children.
Grant us faith, O Christ, to see your presence among us,
so that all creation may sing new songs of gladness
and walk in the way of peace. Amen.

OR

We bless you, Abba, Father,
for you have visited your people
in one like us in all things but sin,
and in human fragility you have revealed
the face of divinity.
Gather into your arms
all the peoples of the world,
so that in your embrace
we may find blessing, peace,
and the fullness of our inheritance
as your daughters and sons. Amen.

Nativity of the Lord
Christmas Day

Any of the following three propers may be used on Christmas Eve/Day.

The readings from propers II and III for Christmas may be used as alternatives for Christmas Day. If proper III is not used on Christmas Day, it should be used at some service during the Christmas cycle because of the significance of John's prologue.

Christmas, Proper I

Thematic

See the seasonal options on p. 38.

Intercessory

With the angels of heaven we proclaim your glory, O God.
As the radiance of your presence lights up the heavens,
we pray for enlightenment
for your church on behalf of the whole world.

Prayers of the People, concluding with:

Grant that, through our prayers,
our lives may radiate the presence of Christ
to all who dwell on earth,
for he is our Lord for ever and ever. Amen.

Scripture

YEAR A, B, C
Isaiah 9:2-7
Psalm 96
Titus 2:11-14
Luke 2:1-14, [15-20]

God of all ages,
in the birth of Christ
your boundless love for your people
shattered the power of darkness.
Be born in us with that same love and light,
that our song may blend with all the choirs of heaven and earth
to the glory of your holy name. Amen.

Christmas, Proper II

Thematic

See the seasonal options on p. 38.

Intercessory

God of incarnation,
your angel host announces
that peace has been born among us,
embodied in fragile flesh.
With confidence in the power of that miracle,
we bring before you our prayers for the church and the world.

Prayers of the People, concluding with:

By your grace, transform our prayers from words to deeds,
that we may live as a holy people
in the dawn of your peace,
redeemed from all that divides us. Amen.

Scripture

YEAR A, B, C
Isaiah 62:6-12
Psalm 97
Titus 3:4-7
Luke 2:[1-7], 8-20

Christ, our God,
whom humble shepherds worshiped at a manger,
you are holy and most high, merciful and mighty.
Startle us to wakefulness,
that we may rejoice in your new and glorious dawn,
and, in your holy name,
act to mend this suffering world. Amen.

OR

Tender and precious God,
from ancient times
the promise of your salvation
has sustained your people.
With Mary and Joseph,
teach us to treasure in our hearts the birth of Jesus,
and with shepherds and angels,
lead us to praise his holy name. Amen.

Christmas, Proper III

Thematic

See the seasonal options on p. 38.

Intercessory

May our gracious God,
whose light shines in the darkness of our lives,
the One who formed creation,
now hear the prayers we offer this day for all people.

Prayers of the People, concluding with:

Splendor of eternal glory,
grant that we may be faithful witnesses
to the light that dawns this morning [day],
proclaiming Christ's word of peace and salvation
in acts of justice and mercy. Amen.

Scripture

YEAR A, B, C
Isaiah 52:7-10
Psalm 98
Hebrews 1:1-4, [5-12]
John 1:1-14

God,
you spoke and your Word became flesh,
breathing a new song of joy and praise
into the world.
Grant that we may bear the good news of your salvation,
proclaiming your promise of peace
to the ends of the earth. Amen.

First Sunday after Christmas Day

Thematic

See the seasonal options on p. 38.

Intercessory

Nurturing God,
remembering the exile of the holy family
and Herod's slaughter of the children,
we remember all who need our sustaining love.
Hear our prayers for the church and the community in the world.

Prayers of the People, concluding with:

Grant that all people may hear together the song of joy,
and find their homes in the garden of justice and hope,
that we may experience the fullness of life,
which is your will for all,
in the coming of Jesus Christ our Lord. Amen.

Scripture

YEAR A
Isaiah 63:7-9
Psalm 148
Hebrews 2:10-18
Matthew 2:13-23

Praise is our cry, O Holy One of Israel,
for you have come among us and borne our burdens.
Give us open hearts,
that we might embrace our suffering sisters and brothers,
and welcome Jesus in the hospitality
we show to exiles. Amen.

YEAR B
Isaiah 61:10—62:3
Psalm 148
Galatians 4:4-7
Luke 2:22-40

God of glory,
you have given us a new name and robed us in salvation.
May we like Anna find our home in your presence,
and like Simeon recognize Jesus as the Christ,
so that, in joy and thanksgiving at becoming your children,
we may join with all creation to sing your praise. Amen.

From our mother's womb you have known us, O God.
You call us to follow you through all our days
and seek us even when we wander.
As we advance in years,
clothe us with your love,
that we may grow in grace and find favor in your sight;
through Jesus Christ. Amen.

Holy Name of Jesus

(Mary, Mother of God)
January 1

Thematic

See the seasonal options on p. 38.

Intercessory

God,
you have claimed us as your people
and entrusted the justice and holiness
of your creation
to our hands and hearts.
Hear the prayers we offer this day
on behalf of this world.

Prayers of the People, concluding with:

Grant that we may not only pray with our lips,
but be courageous in conduct,
responding to your grace
with faithful and fruitful action. Amen.

Scripture

YEAR A, B, C
Numbers 6:22-27
Psalm 8
Galatians 4:4-7 *or* Philippians 2:5-11
Luke 2:15-21

O God of ancient blessing,
your servant Mary pondered in her heart
the treasured words spoken about her Son,
our Savior Jesus Christ.
Prepare our hearts to receive his Spirit,
that our tongues may confess him Lord. Amen.

New Year's Day
January 1

Thematic

God of new beginnings,
you wipe away our tears
and call us to care for one another.
Give us eyes to see your gifts,
hearts to embrace all creation,
and hands to serve you every day of our lives.
We ask this in the name of Jesus. Amen.

Intercessory

At the beginning of this new year,
we implore God's blessing upon our work
and pray for the needs of this new year of grace.

Prayers of the People, concluding with:

Throughout all time you have blessed your people, O God,
and dwelt among them.
On the eve [first day] of this new year,
inspire and guide us,
that all we do may find in you its beginning and fulfillment. Amen.

Scripture

YEAR A, B, C
Ecclesiastes 3:1-13
Psalm 8
Revelation 21:1-6a
Matthew 25:31-46

How majestic your name in all the earth, O Lord our Sovereign!
The heavens reflect your glory
and the earth proclaims the wonder of your loving care.
In the fullness of time you crowned creation
with the birth of your Son.
Continue your work of salvation among us
and form us into a new creation
that, as we behold the vision of a new heaven and a new earth,
we may sing your glory. Amen.

Second Sunday after Christmas Day

The following prayers and readings are provided for use when Epiphany (January 6) is celebrated on a weekday following the Second Sunday after Christmas Day.

Thematic

See the seasonal options on p. 38.

Intercessory

God has blessed creation with a great variety of gifts
and gathered all people into one family,
so that in sharing, we might strengthen
and be strengthened by one another.
We gather into our hearts and minds
the universe entrusted to us,
remembering its needs before God and this company.

Prayers of the People, concluding with:

Grant that these prayers, O God,
may be enfleshed by our commitment not only to pray them,
but to live them in your Son's name. Amen.

Scripture

YEAR A, B, C
Jeremiah 31:7-14 *or* Sirach 24:1-12
Psalm 147:12-20 *or* Wisdom of Solomon 10:15-21
Ephesians 1:3-14
John 1:[1-9], 10-18

Gracious God,
you have redeemed us through Jesus Christ,
the first-born of all creation,
whose birth we celebrate as the child of Bethlehem.
Bless us with every spiritual blessing,
that we may live as your adopted children
and witness to your glory
with unending praise and thanksgiving. Amen.

Epiphany

Seasonal Prayers

Thematic

Perfect Light of revelation,
as you shone in the life of Jesus,
whose epiphany we celebrate,
so shine in us and through us,
that we may become beacons of truth and compassion,
enlightening all creation
with deeds of justice and mercy. Amen.

OR

O God,
you spoke your word
and revealed your good news in Jesus, the Christ.
Fill all creation with that word again,
so that by proclaiming your joyful promises to all nations
and singing of your glorious hope to all peoples,
we may become one living body,
your incarnate presence on the earth. Amen.

Intercessory

To God who welcomes all in love,
let us pray for the good of the church
and the concerns of those in need.

Prayers of the People, concluding with:

God of every land and nation,
you have created all people
and you dwell among us in Jesus Christ.
Listen to the cries of those who pray to you,
and grant that, as we proclaim the greatness of your name,
all people will know the power of love at work in the world.
We ask this through Christ our Lord. Amen.

OR

Sisters and brothers,
let us lift our hearts in faith
to the one who hears all prayers
and holds close all those in need.

Prayers of the People, concluding with:

Holy God, you gather the whole universe
into your radiant presence
and continually reveal your Son as our Savior.
Bring healing to all wounds,
make whole all that is broken,
speak truth to all illusion,
and shed light in every darkness,
that all creation will see your glory and know your Christ. Amen.

Epiphany of the Lord

Thematic

O God of light and peace,
whose glory, shining in the child of Bethlehem,
still draws the nations to yourself:
dispel the darkness that shrouds our path,
that we may come
to kneel before Christ in true worship,
offer him our hearts and souls,
and return from his presence to live as he has taught. Amen.

Intercessory

God of revelation,
as we gather in praise for the gracious mystery of your Son,
we remember the many needs of your church and your world.

Prayers of the People, concluding with:

Guide us on the path of salvation, O God,
that the radiance and power of your Holy Spirit
working in the world
will gather together all peoples and nations in one community
to offer you worship and proclaim your splendor. Amen.

Scripture

Year A, B, C
Isaiah 60:1-6
Psalm 72:1-7, 10-14
Ephesians 3:1-12
Matthew 2:1-12

Radiant Morning Star,
you are both guidance and mystery.
Visit our rest with disturbing dreams,
and our journeys with strange companions.
Grace us with the hospitality
to open our hearts and homes
to visitors filled with unfamiliar wisdom
bearing profound and unusual gifts. Amen.

OR

Bright Morning Star,
your light has come,
and the birth of Jesus
has overwhelmed us with joy.
Like the magi of long ago,
may we be drawn to you
and offer you such gifts as we are able. Amen.

Baptism of the Lord [1]
First Sunday after the Epiphany

Thematic

God of grace and glory,
you call us with your voice of flame
to be your people, faithful and courageous.
As your beloved Son
embraced his mission in the waters of baptism,
inspire us with the fire of your Spirit
to join in his transforming work.
We ask this in the name of our Savior Jesus Christ,
who lives and reigns for ever and ever. Amen.

Intercessory

Sisters and brothers,
our baptismal vows call us to compassion and mercy
on behalf of those in need.
We offer our prayers for the church and the world.

Prayers of the People, concluding with:

Lord God,
you revealed your Son in the waters of the Jordan
and anointed him with the power of the Holy Spirit
to proclaim good news to all people.
Sanctify us by the same Spirit,
that we may proclaim the healing power of the gospel
by acts of love in your name. Amen.

Scripture

Year A
Isaiah 42:1-9
Psalm 29
Acts 10:34-43
Matthew 3:13-17

Creator God, our soul's delight,
your voice thunders over the waters,
liberating the future from the past.
In the Spirit's power and the waters of rebirth,
Jesus was declared your blessed and beloved Son;
may we recall our baptism,
and be disciples of the Anointed One. Amen.

Holy God,
creator of light and herald of goodness,
at the waters of his baptism
you proclaimed Jesus your beloved Son.
With the baptized of every time and generation,
may we say yes to your call to repentance
and be led to the life of abundance we experience
in your kinship and your love. Amen.

God, your voice moves over the waters.
Immerse us in your grace,
mark us with your image,
and raise us to live our baptismal vows
empowered by the Holy Spirit
and the example of Christ our Lord,
in whose name we pray. Amen.

Second Sunday after the Epiphany [2]

Thematic

See the seasonal options on p. 50.

Intercessory

See the seasonal options on p. 51.

Scripture

Year A

Isaiah 49:1-7
Psalm 40:1-11
I Corinthians 1:1-9
John 1:29-42

Steadfast God,
you have enriched and enlightened us
by the revelation of your eternal Christ.
Comfort us in our mortality
and strengthen us
to walk the path of your desire,
so that by word and deed we may manifest
the gracious news of your faithfulness and love. Amen.

Year B

1 Samuel 3:1-10, [11-20]
Psalm 139:1-6, 13-18
I Corinthians 6:12-20
John 1:43-51

Insistent God,
by night and day you summon your slumbering people.
So stir us with your voice
and enlighten our lives with your grace
that we give ourselves fully
to Christ's call to mission and ministry. Amen.

Year C
Isaiah 62:1-5
Psalm 36:5-10
1 Corinthians 12:1-11
John 2:1-11

O God of steadfast love,
at the wedding in Cana
your Son Jesus turned water into wine,
delighting all who were there.
Transform our hearts by your Spirit,
that we may use our varied gifts
to show forth the light of your love
as one body in Christ. Amen.

Third Sunday after the Epiphany [3]

Thematic

See the seasonal options on p. 50.

Intercessory

See the seasonal options on p. 51.

Scripture

Year A
Isaiah 9:1-4
Psalm 27:1, 4-9
I Corinthians 1:10-18
Matthew 4:12-23

God of blazing light,
through the power of the cross you shattered our darkness,
scattering the fears that bind us
and setting us free to live as your children.
Give us courage and conviction
that we may joyfully turn and follow you
into new adventures of faithful service,
led by the light that shines
through Jesus Christ our Savior. Amen.

Year B
Jonah 3:1-5, 10
Psalm 62:5-12
1 Corinthians 7:29-31
Mark 1:14-20

God of the prophets,
you call us from evil to serve you.
Fulfill in us your commonwealth of justice and joy,
that the light of your presence
may be revealed to all nations,
to the glory of Jesus' name. Amen.

Year C
Nehemiah 8:1-3, 5-6, 8-10
Psalm 19
1 Corinthians 12:12-31a
Luke 4:14-21

In you, O Lord our God,
we find our joy,
for through your law and your prophets
you formed a people in mercy and freedom,
in justice and righteousness.
Pour your Spirit on us today,
that we who are Christ's body
may bear the good news of your ancient promises
to all who seek you. Amen.

Fourth Sunday after the Epiphany [4]

If this Sunday immediately precedes Ash Wednesday, this proper may be replaced, in those churches using Transfiguration readings on this day, by the readings for the Last Sunday after the Epiphany.

Thematic

See the seasonal options on p. 50.

Intercessory

See the seasonal options on p. 51.

Scripture

Year A
Micah 6:1-8
Psalm 15
1 Corinthians 1:18-31
Matthew 5:1-12

God our deliverer,
you walk with the meek and the poor,
the compassionate and those who mourn,
and you call us to walk humbly with you.
When we are foolish, be our wisdom;
when we are weak, be our strength;
that, as we learn to do justice
and to love mercy,
your rule may come as blessing. Amen.

Year B
Deuteronomy 18:15-20
Psalm 111
1 Corinthians 8:1-13
Mark 1:21-28

Holy and awesome God,
your Son's authority is found in integrity and living truth,
not the assertion of power over others.
Open our imaginations to new dimensions of your love,
and heal us of all that severs us from you and one another,
that we may grow into the vision you unfold before us. Amen.

Year C
Jeremiah 1:4-10
Psalm 71:1-6
1 Corinthians 13:1-13
Luke 4:21-30

O God of all the prophets,
you knew us and chose us
before you formed us in the womb.
Fill us with faith that speaks your word,
hope that does not disappoint,
and love that bears all things for your sake,
until that day when we shall know you fully,
even as we are known by you. Amen.

Fifth Sunday after the Epiphany [5]

If this Sunday immediately precedes Ash Wednesday, this proper may be replaced, in those churches using Transfiguration readings on this day, by the readings for the Last Sunday after the Epiphany.

Thematic

See the seasonal options on p. 50.

Intercessory

See the seasonal options on p. 51.

Scripture

Year A
Isaiah 58:1-9a, [9b-12]
Psalm 112:1-9, [10]
1 Corinthians 2:1-12, [13-16]
Matthew 5:13-20

O God of light,
your searching Spirit reveals and illumines
your presence in creation.
Shine your radiant holiness into our lives,
that we may offer our hands and hearts to your work:
to heal and shelter,
to feed and clothe,
to break every yoke and silence evil tongues. Amen.

Year B
Isaiah 40:21-31
Psalm 147:1-11, 20c
1 Corinthians 9:16-23
Mark 1:29-39

Everlasting God,
you give strength to the powerless
and power to the faint;
you raise up the sick
and cast out demons.
Make us agents of healing and wholeness,
that your good news may be made known
to the ends of your creation. Amen.

Year C
Isaiah 6:1-8, [9-13]
Psalm 138
1 Corinthians 15:1-11
Luke 5:1-11

Loving God,
you have called forth disciples and prophets
to live and speak your word.
Give us ears to hear,
lives to respond,
and voices to proclaim the good news of salvation,
which we know in our Savior Jesus Christ,
who lives and reigns with you and the Holy Spirit,
one God, now and forever. Amen.

Sixth Sunday after the Epiphany [6]

Proper 1

If this Sunday immediately precedes Ash Wednesday, this proper may be replaced, in those churches using Transfiguration readings on this day, by the readings for the Last Sunday after the Epiphany.

Thematic

See the seasonal options on p. 50.

Intercessory

See the seasonal options on p. 51.

Scripture

Year A
Deuteronomy 30:15-20 *or* Sirach 15:15-20
Psalm 119:1-8
1 Corinthians 3:1-9
Matthew 5:21-37

Divine Gardener,
you give growth to our seeds
and to the towering forest trees;
you raise to abundant life that which seems dead.
Teach us to choose blessing
and life rather than death,
so that we may walk blamelessly,
seeking you
through reconciliation with all of your children. Amen.

Divine Physician,
healer of bodies and souls,
stretch out your hand and touch us.
Cleanse our hearts from the sin
that separates us from you and one another.
Recreate us in your own image,
and restore us in Christ,
so that we may run the race
and receive the prize of everlasting life. Amen.

Year C
Jeremiah 17:5-10
Psalm 1
1 Corinthians 15:12-20
Luke 6:17-26

God, you root those who trust in you
by streams of healing water.
Release us from the bonds of disease,
free us from the power of evil,
and turn us from falsehood and illusion,
that we may find the blessing of new life in you
through the power of Christ. Amen.

Seventh Sunday after the Epiphany [7]

Proper 2

If this Sunday immediately precedes Ash Wednesday, this proper may be replaced, in those churches using Transfiguration readings on this day, by the readings for the Last Sunday after the Epiphany.

Thematic

See the seasonal options on p. 50.

Intercessory

See the seasonal options on p. 51.

Scripture

Year A
Leviticus 19:1-2, 9-18
Psalm 119:33-40
1 Corinthians 3:10-11, 16-23
Matthew 5:38-48

O God most holy,
in Jesus Christ you have laid a foundation
upon which to build our lives.
Help us to follow your perfect law of love,
that we may fulfill it
and observe it to the end. Amen.

Year B
Isaiah 43:18-25
Psalm 41
2 Corinthians 1:18-22
Mark 2:1-12

Faithful God,
the fulfillment of your promise in Christ
has brought new life to all creation:
the forgiveness of sins and our restoration to wholeness.
Anoint us with your Spirit
that we may be alert and mindful ministers
of your gracious will to save,
and persevere in bringing into your presence
all that is broken and in need of healing,
through Jesus Christ, our Lord. Amen.

Year C
Genesis 45:3-11, 15
Psalm 37:1-11, 39-40
1 Corinthians 15:35-38, 42-50
Luke 6:27-38

O perfect Love,
whose compassionate power transforms sin into health
and temporal dust into eternal glory:
grant us a gracious faith,
so that like Joseph, when he was sold into slavery,
we may face our trials with confidence,
and become a blessing
to friend and enemy alike in Jesus' name. Amen.

Eighth Sunday after the Epiphany [8]

Proper 3

If this Sunday immediately precedes Ash Wednesday, this proper may be replaced, in those churches using Transfiguration readings on this day, by the readings for the Last Sunday after the Epiphany.

Thematic

See the seasonal options on p. 50.

Intercessory

See the seasonal options on p. 51.

Scripture

Year A

Isaiah 49:8-16a
Psalm 131
1 Corinthians 4:1-5
Matthew 6:24-34

God of tender care,
like a mother you never forget your children,
but comfort and quiet those who are restless and fearful;
like a father you know already what we need.
In all our anxiety, give us the spirit of trust;
in all our worry, give us faithful hearts;
that in confidence and calm
we may seek the kingdom of Christ
where your holy will of peace and justice
has been made known. Amen.

Year B

Hosea 2:14-20
Psalm 103:1-13, 22
2 Corinthians 3:1-6
Mark 2:13-22

Holy lover of Israel,
hopeful spouse to a people,
with tender words and covenant promise
you invite us to meet your love with faithfulness.
May we live with you
in righteousness and justice,
in steadfast love and mercy,
to your glory for ever. Amen.

From your mouth, O God,
come mercy and righteousness,
and out of the abundance of your heart
you have given us your Word made flesh, Jesus the Christ.
Pour out your Spirit of integrity upon us,
that all we say and do
may befit a people made in your image
and baptized into the dying and rising of your Son. Amen.

Ninth Sunday after the Epiphany [9]

Proper 4

The readings that follow are for churches whose calendar requires this Sunday, and do not observe the Last Sunday after the Epiphany as Transfiguration.

Thematic

See the seasonal options on p. 50.

Intercessory

See the seasonal options on p. 51.

Scripture

Year A

Deuteronomy 11:18-21, 26-28
Psalm 31:1-5, 19-24
Romans 1:16-17; 3:22b-28, [29-31]
Matthew 7:21-29

O Lord, faithful God,
you are our rock and our refuge.
Help us to hear your word as truth
and to act on it in faith,
that all may come to know your love. Amen.

Year B

Deuteronomy 5:12-15
Psalm 81:1-10
2 Corinthians 4:5-12
Mark 2:23—3:6

On this day of rest and gladness,
we praise you, God of creation,
for the dignity of work and the joy of play,
for the challenge of witness
and the invitation to delight at your table.
Renew our hearts through your sabbath rest,
that we might be refreshed
to continue in your work
of restoring the world to wholeness. Amen.

The greatness of your deeds, Lord God,
declares your love for all people
and shows forth the glory of your name.
Teach us to welcome both our neighbor
and the stranger in our midst,
that all may know the healing touch of your Son,
who announces the good news of salvation
in word and deed. Amen.

Last Sunday after the Epiphany

Transfiguration Sunday

The following may be used in churches where the last Sunday after the Epiphany is observed as Transfiguration Sunday.

Thematic

Holy God, mighty and immortal,
you are beyond our knowing,
yet we see your glory in the face of Jesus Christ,
whose compassion illumines the world.
Transform us into the likeness of the love of Christ,
who renewed our humanity so that we may share in his divinity,
the same Jesus Christ, our Lord,
who lives and reigns with you and the Holy Spirit. Amen.

Intercessory

O God, as your Son drew apart
to be in prayer with you,
we offer our prayers
for the transformation of the world and the church.

Prayers of the People, concluding with:

You revealed your glory and presence
in your beloved Son, Jesus the Christ.
In receiving our prayers,
reveal the glory and presence of your Spirit
alive in the world today,
free us from all doubts,
and empower us to act as a transfigured people. Amen.

Scripture

Year A
Exodus 24:12-18
Psalm 2 *or* Psalm 99
2 Peter 1:16-21
Matthew 17:1-9

O God of the covenant,
the cloud of your splendor and the fire of your love
revealed your Son on the mountain heights.
Transform our lives in his image,
write your law of love on our hearts,
and make us prophets of your glory,
that we may lead others into your presence. Amen.

Year B
2 Kings 2:1-12
Psalm 50:1-6
2 Corinthians 4:3-6
Mark 9:2-9

Holy God,
you have revealed the glory of your love in Jesus Christ,
and have given us a share in your Spirit.
May we who listen to Christ
follow faithfully,
and, in the dark places where you send us,
reveal the light of your gospel. Amen.

Year C
Exodus 34:29-35
Psalm 99
2 Corinthians 3:12—4:2
Luke 9:28-36, [37-43]

Eternal God,
you revealed to the disciples
the everlasting glory of Jesus Christ.
Grant us, who have not seen and yet believe,
the gift of your Holy Spirit,
that we may boldly live the gospel
and shine with your transforming glory,
as people changed and changing
through the redeeming presence of our Savior. Amen.

Lent

Seasonal Prayers

Thematic

God of wilderness and water,
your Son was baptized and tempted as we are.
Guide us through this season,
that we may not avoid struggle,
but open ourselves to blessing,
through the cleansing depths of repentance
and the heaven-rending words of the Spirit. Amen.

OR

Artist of souls,
you sculpted a people for yourself
out of the rocks of wilderness and fasting.
Help us as we take up your invitation to prayer and simplicity,
that the discipline of these forty days
may sharpen our hunger for the feast of your holy friendship,
and whet our thirst for the living water you offer
through Jesus Christ. Amen.

OR

God of the covenant,
in the glory of the cross
your Son embraced the power of death
and broke its hold over your people.
In this time of repentance,
draw all people to yourself,
that we who confess Jesus as Lord
may put aside the deeds of death
and accept the life of your kingdom. Amen.

OR

God of the living,
through baptism we pass from the shadow of death
to the light of the resurrection.
Remain with us and give us hope
that, rejoicing in the gift of the Spirit
who gives life to our mortal flesh,
we may be clothed with the garment of immortality,
through Jesus Christ our Lord. Amen.

Ash Wednesday

Thematic

Righteous God,
in humility and repentance
we bring our failures in caring, helping, and loving,
we bring the pain we have caused others,
we bring the injustice in society of which we are a part,
to the transforming power of your grace.
Grant us the courage to accept the healing you offer
and to turn again toward the sunrise of your reign,
that we may walk with you in the promise of peace
you have willed for all the children of the earth,
and have made known to us in Christ Jesus. Amen.

Intercessory

Gracious and merciful God,
you see into the secret places of our hearts,
where we mourn our sins.
As we turn again to your grace, receive our prayers.

Prayers of the People, concluding with:

Look with mercy on our contrite hearts,
wash from us the stain of iniquity,
and create a new and right spirit in us,
that we may declare your praise
and offer an acceptable sacrifice in these Lenten days;
through Christ Jesus, who bore our sins on the cross. Amen.

Scripture

YEAR A, B, C
Joel 2:1-2, 12-17 *or* Isaiah 58:1-12
Psalm 51:1-17
2 Corinthians 5:20b—6:10
Matthew 6:1-6, 16-21

O God, you delight not in pomp and show,
but in a humble and contrite heart.
Overturn our love of worldly possessions
and fix our hearts more firmly on you,
that, having nothing,
we may yet possess everything,
a treasure stored up for us in heaven. Amen.

First Sunday in Lent

Thematic

See the seasonal options on p. 76.

Intercessory

Beloved friends, in this season of repentance and healing,
we accept God's invitation to be ever-mindful of the needs of others,
offering our prayers on behalf of God's community in the church and the world.

Prayers of the People, concluding with:

Fill us with your strength
to resist the seductions of our foolish desires
and the tempter's vain delights,
that we may walk in obedience and righteousness,
rejoicing in you with an upright heart. Amen.

Scripture

YEAR A
Genesis 2:15-17; 3:1-7
Psalm 32
Romans 5:12-19
Matthew 4:1-11

God of mercy,
your word was the sure defense of Jesus in his time of testing.
Minister to us in the wilderness of our temptation,
that we who have been set free from sin by Christ
may serve you well into life everlasting. Amen.

YEAR B
Genesis 9:8-17
Psalm 25:1-10
1 Peter 3:18-22
Mark 1:9-15

God of our salvation,
your bow in the clouds
proclaims your covenant with every living creature.
Teach us your paths and lead us in your truth,
that by your Holy Spirit,
we may remember our baptismal vows
and be keepers of your trust with earth and its inhabitants. Amen.

YEAR C
Deuteronomy 26:1-11
Psalm 91:1-2, 9-16
Romans 10:8b-13
Luke 4:1-13

God of deliverance and freedom,
you taught the people of Israel
to acknowledge that all things
come from your bountiful hand.
Deepen our faith
so that we may resist temptation
and, in the midst of trial,
proclaim that Jesus Christ is Lord,
now and for ever. Amen.

Second Sunday in Lent

Thematic

See the seasonal options on p. 76.

Intercessory

God of the covenant,
you call us to be
fruitful servants within creation,
and to offer our lives
as the foundation of your realm.
We lay before you the desires of our hearts,
that we may be transformed by their fulfillment.

Prayers of the People, concluding with:

Grant, O God, that the prayers we offer
may be your channel for new and abundant life
not only hoped for,
but worked for,
through faithful word and deed. Amen.

Scripture

YEAR A
Genesis 12:1-4a
Psalm 121
Romans 4:1-5, 13-17
John 3:1-17 *or* Matthew 17:1-9

God of amazing compassion,
lover of our wayward race,
you bring to birth a pilgrim people,
and call us to be a blessing for ourselves and all the world.
We pray for grace to take your generous gift
and step with courage on this holy path,
confident in the radiant life that is your plan for us,
made known and given in Jesus Christ our Lord. Amen.

YEAR B
Genesis 17:1-7, 15-16
Psalm 22:23-31
Romans 4:13-25
Mark 8:31-38 *or* Mark 9:2-9

God of Sarah and Abraham,
long ago you embraced your people in covenant
and promised them your blessing.
Strengthen us in faith,
that, with your disciples of every age,
we may proclaim your deliverance in Jesus Christ
to generations yet unborn. Amen.

YEAR C
Genesis 15:1-12, 17-18
Psalm 27
Philippians 3:17—4:1
Luke 13:31-35 *or* Luke 9:28-36

Hope beyond all human hope,
you promised descendants as numerous as the stars
to old Abraham and barren Sarah.
You promise light and salvation
in the midst of darkness and despair,
and promise redemption to a world that will not listen.
Gather us to yourself in tenderness,
open our ears to listen to your word,
and teach us to live faithfully
as people confident of the fulfillment of your promises.
We ask this in the name of Jesus Christ. Amen.

Third Sunday in Lent

Thematic

See the seasonal options on p. 76.

Intercessory

Faithful God of love,
you blessed us with your servant Son
so that we might know how to serve your people
with justice and with mercy.
We gather the needs of ourselves and others,
and offer them to you in faith and love,
seeking to be strengthened to meet them.

Prayers of the People, concluding with:

Shape us and transform us by your grace,
that we may grow in wisdom and in confidence,
never faltering until we have done all that you desire
to bring your realm of shalom to fulfillment. Amen.

Scripture

YEAR A
Exodus 17:1-7
Psalm 95
Romans 5:1-11
John 4:5-42

Enduring Presence,
goal and guide,
you go before and await our coming.
Only our thirst compels us
beyond complaint to conversation,
beyond rejection to relationship.
Pour your love into our hearts,
that, refreshed and renewed,
we may invite others to the living water
given to us in Jesus Christ our Lord. Amen.

Holy One, creator of the stars and seas,
your steadfast love is shown to every living thing:
your word calls forth countless worlds and souls;
your law revives and refreshes.
Forgive our misuse of your gifts,
that we may be transformed by your wisdom
to manifest for others
the mercy of our crucified and risen Lord. Amen.

God of infinite goodness,
throughout the ages you have persevered
in claiming and reclaiming your people.
Renew for us your call to repentance,
surround us with witnesses to aid us in our journey,
and grant us the time to fashion our lives anew,
through Jesus Christ our Savior. Amen.

Fourth Sunday in Lent

Thematic

See the seasonal options on p. 76.

Intercessory

My brothers and sisters:
reconciled to God by the mercy of Christ,
we pray with confidence for the needs of the church and the world.

Prayers of the People, concluding with:

Through Christ you make us a new creation, O God,
for with him we pass from sin to the new life of grace.
Accept our prayers in the warm embrace of your compassion,
and welcome all people to the festive banquet of your table,
where we may rejoice in your love
and celebrate the inheritance you have given to us.
We ask this through Jesus Christ our Lord. Amen.

Scripture

YEAR A
1 Samuel 16:1-13
Psalm 23
Ephesians 5:8-14
John 9:1-41

Discerner of hearts,
you look beneath our outward appearance
and see your image in each of us.
Banish in us the blindness
that prevents us from recognizing truth,
so we may see the world through your eyes
and with the compassion of Jesus Christ who redeems us. Amen.

YEAR B
Numbers 21:4-9
Psalm 107:1-3, 17-22
Ephesians 2:1-10
John 3:14-21

Steadfast God,
you reach out to us in mercy
even when we rebel against your holy call
and prefer to walk in disobedience
rather than in the way of your divine truth.
Soften our hearts with the warmth of your love,
that we may know your Son alive within us,
redeeming us
and raising us up into your eternal presence. Amen.

YEAR C
Joshua 5:9-12
Psalm 32
2 Corinthians 5:16-21
Luke 15:1-3, 11b-32

God of patient love,
you await the return of the wayward and wandering
and eagerly embrace them in pardon.
Through baptism you have clothed us with the glory of Christ
and restored our inheritance:
give us generous hearts
to welcome all who seek a place
at the table of your unconditional love.
We ask this through Jesus Christ our Lord. Amen.

OR

Eternal lover of our wayward race,
we praise you for your ever-open door.
You open your arms to accept us
even before we turn to meet your welcome;
you invite us to forgiveness
even before our hearts are softened to repentance.
Hold before us the image of our humanity made new,
that we may live in Jesus Christ,
the model and the pioneer of your new creation. Amen.

Fifth Sunday in Lent

Thematic

See the seasonal options on p. 76.

Intercessory

Sisters and brothers,
as Jesus, in the days before his passion,
offered prayers and supplications with loud cries and tears,
let us pray for those who suffer, those who are in need,
and those who seek reconciliation.

Prayers of the People, concluding with:

God of compassion,
you know our faults and yet you promise to forgive.
Keep us in your presence and give us your wisdom.
Open our hearts to gladness,
call dry bones to dance,
and restore to us the joy of your salvation. Amen.

Scripture

YEAR A
Ezekiel 37:1-14
Psalm 130
Romans 8:6-11
John 11:1-45

God of all consolation and compassion,
your Son comforted the grieving sisters, Martha and Mary;
your breath alone brings life
to dry bones and weary souls.
Pour out your Spirit upon us,
that we may face despair and death
with the hope of resurrection
and faith in the One
who called Lazarus forth from the grave. Amen.

YEAR B
Jeremiah 31:31-34
Psalm 51:1-12 *or* Psalm 119:9-16
Hebrews 5:5-10
John 12:20-33

God of suffering and glory,
in Jesus Christ you reveal the way of life
through the path of obedience.
Inscribe your law in our hearts,
that in life we may not stray from you,
but may be your people. Amen.

YEAR C
Isaiah 43:16-21
Psalm 126
Philippians 3:4b-14
John 12:1-8

Creator God,
you prepare a new way in the wilderness
and your grace waters the desert.
Help us to recognize your hand
working miracles beyond our imagining.
Open our hearts to be transformed
by the new thing you are doing,
so that our lives may proclaim
the extravagance of your love for all,
and its presence in Jesus Christ. Amen.

Sixth Sunday in Lent

Passion Sunday

When the procession with palms is observed, the gospel and psalm from the Palm Sunday set of readings (pp. 90–91) may be used in the Liturgy of the Palms.

Whenever possible, the whole passion narrative should be read.

Thematic

See the seasonal options on p. 76.

Intercessory

Caught between joy and despair,
we yearn for the fulfillment of God's desire
beyond the brokenness and neediness of this life.
We offer thanksgiving for God's presence with us
and petitions for the transformation
of the church and the world.

Prayers of the People, concluding with:

Life-giver, Pain-bearer, Love-maker,
day by day you sustain the weary with your word
and gently encourage us to place our trust in you.
Awaken us to the suffering of those around us;
save us from hiding in denials or taunts that deepen the hurt;
give us grace to share one another's burdens in humble service. Amen.

Scripture

YEAR A
Isaiah 50:4-9a
Psalm 31:9-16
Philippians 2:5-11
Matthew 26:14—27:66 *or* Matthew 27:11-54

Merciful God,
your strength and courage pour forth
to sustain the witness of your faithful people.
Awaken in us the humility to serve
wherever creation is broken and in need,
that we may follow in the way of our brother, Jesus,
die as he did to all that separates us from you,
and with him be raised to new life. Amen.

YEAR B
Isaiah 50:4-9a
Psalm 31:9-16
Philippians 2:5-11
Mark 14:1—15:47
or Mark 15:1-39, [40-47]

Crucified and Risen One,
by your passion
you sustain us when we fall
knee-bent into the radical emptiness
of bone-wasting sorrow and despair.
Teach us to sustain the weary
and awaken us to attend to those who suffer. Amen.

YEAR C
Isaiah 50:4-9a
Psalm 31:9-16
Philippians 2:5-11
Luke 22:14—23:56 *or* Luke 23:1-49

Compassionate God,
your love finds full expression
in the gift of Jesus Christ your Son,
who willingly met betrayal and death
to set us free from sin.
Give us courage to live obediently in these days
until we greet the glory of our risen Savior. Amen.

Sixth Sunday in Lent
Palm Sunday

Thematic

See the seasonal options on p. 76.

Intercessory

Caught between joy and despair,
we yearn for the fulfillment of God's desire
beyond the brokenness and neediness of this life.
We offer thanksgiving for God's presence with us
and petitions for the transformation
of the church and the world.

Prayers of the People, concluding with:

Life-giver, Pain-bearer, Love-maker,
day by day you sustain the weary with your word
and gently encourage us to place our trust in you.
Awaken us to the suffering of those around us;
save us from hiding in denials or taunts that deepen the hurt;
give us grace to share one another's burdens in humble service. Amen.

Scripture

YEAR A
Isaiah 50:4-9a
Psalm 118:1-2, 19-29
Philippians 2:5-11
Matthew 21:1-11

God of our salvation,
we give you thanks for Jesus Christ, our Lord,
who came in your name
and turned the lonely way of rejection and death
into triumph.
Grant us the steadfast faith
to enter the gates of righteousness,
that we may receive grace to become worthy citizens
of your holy realm. Amen.

YEAR B
Isaiah 50:4-9a
Psalm 118:1-2, 19-29
Philippians 2:5-11
Mark 11:1-11 or John 12:12-16

Sovereign God,
you have established your rule over the human heart,
not by force
but by the servant example of Jesus Christ.
Move us by your Spirit
to join the joyful procession
of those who confess Christ Jesus with their tongues
and praise him with their lives. Amen.

YEAR C
Isaiah 50:4-9a
Psalm 118:1-2, 19-29
Philippians 2:5-11
Luke 19:28-40

Giver of light,
your steadfast love endures forever.
Open our hearts to the Blessed One who comes so humbly,
on a borrowed colt.
Open before us the gates of your justice,
that we may enter,
confessing in heaven and on earth
that Jesus is Lord. Amen.

Holy Week
Three Days

Seasonal Prayers

Thematic

Almighty God,
your name is glorified
even in the anguish of your Son's death.
Grant us the courage
to receive your anointed servant
who embodies a wisdom and love
that is foolishness to the world.
Empower us in witness
so that all the world may recognize
in the scandal of the cross
the mystery of reconciliation. Amen.

OR

Faithful Midwife,
as you delivered the Hebrews safely
out of the long labor of slavery,
so, morning by morning,
you draw us forth into the new day.
Surround us with a cloud of witnesses,
and sustain us by your powerful word,
that, in the night of loneliness and fear,
we, being weary, may not lose heart
but push toward the joy that is to come,
laboring with Christ
to give birth to your promised kingdom. Amen.

OR

Creator of the universe,
you made the world in beauty,
and restore all things in glory
through the victory of Jesus Christ.
We pray that, wherever your image is still disfigured
by poverty, sickness, selfishness, war, and greed,
the new creation in Jesus Christ may appear in justice, love, and peace,
to the glory of your name. Amen.

OR

Christ our God,
your love is poured out in death for our sakes.
Hold us in your embrace
as we wait for Easter's dawn.
Comfort us with the promise
that no power on earth, not even death itself,
can separate us from your love;
and strengthen us to wait
until you are revealed to us
in all your risen glory. Amen.

Monday of Holy Week

Thematic

See the seasonal options on pp. 94–95.

Intercessory

God, through Christ, has given us as a covenant to the people,
to heal and to liberate through prayer and work.
We gather the concerns of the church and the world,
and hold them in our hearts before our creator and redeemer.

Prayers of the People, concluding with:

Gracious God, the hope of all in need,
pour your Spirit upon us,
that we may be instruments of your justice and compassion,
a light to the nations,
and a living promise of your new heaven and new earth. Amen.

Scripture

YEAR A, B, C
Isaiah 42:1-9
Psalm 36:5-11
Hebrews 9:11-15
John 12:1-11

God of steadfast love,
light of the blind and liberator of the oppressed,
we see your holy purpose
in the tender compassion of Jesus,
who calls us into new and living friendship with you.
May we, who take shelter in the shadow of your wings,
be filled with the grace of his tender caring;
may we, who stumble in selfish darkness,
see your glory in the light of his self-giving.
We ask this through him whose suffering is victorious,
Jesus Christ our Savior. Amen.

Tuesday of Holy Week

Thematic

See the seasonal options on pp. 94–95.

Intercessory

God our strength,
we lift to you the deepest prayers of our hearts
that you will save us from the time of trial
and comfort us in tribulation.

Prayers of the People, concluding with:

Reveal your glory to the nations,
that your cross may stand
as a sign of the power
that conquers human pride
and confounds the wisdom of this world. Amen.

Scripture

YEAR A, B, C
Isaiah 49:1-7
Psalm 71:1-14
1 Corinthians 1:18-31
John 12:20-36

Holy and immortal God,
from earliest times
you have named us
and called us into discipleship.
Teach us to follow the One
whose light scatters the darkness of our world,
that we may walk as children of the light. Amen.

Wednesday of Holy Week

Thematic

See the seasonal options on pp. 94–95.

Intercessory

Holy God,
who call your people to sustain the weary
and protect the oppressed.
Uphold us in our concern
and strengthen us,
that we may not only speak our prayers
but act on behalf of their fulfillment.

Prayers of the People, concluding with:

Most Holy One,
grant that we may be counted
as members of the great cloud of witnesses
who live with justice and compassion,
and reveal your divine glory before all people. Amen.

Scripture

YEAR A, B, C
Isaiah 50:4-9a
Psalm 70
Hebrews 12:1-3
John 13:21-32

Troubled God,
in every generation
you call your people to contend
against the brutality of sin and betrayal.
Keep us steadfast even in our fear and uncertainty,
that we may follow
where Jesus has led the way. Amen.

Holy Thursday
Maundy Thursday

Thematic

God of the covenant,
as we celebrate the beginning of the paschal feast,
we come to the table of the Lord
in whom we have salvation, life, and resurrection.
Renew the power of this mystery
in our service to one another and to you,
so that with Christ we may pass from this life
to the glory of your kingdom. Amen.

Intercessory

Let us offer our prayers
for the needs of the church and the world
to God who has given us new life
in Christ's passage through death.

Prayers of the People, concluding with:

By the blood of the covenant
and the waters of baptism, O God,
you cleansed us from sin and made us one in Christ.
Receive these prayers that, by the power of your Spirit,
we may love our brothers and sisters
even as Christ has loved us. Amen.

Scripture

YEAR A, B, C
Exodus 12:1-4, [5-10], 11-14
Psalm 116:1-2, 12-19
1 Corinthians 11:23-26
John 13:1-17, 31b-35

Eternal God, in the sharing of a meal
your Son established a new covenant for all people,
and in the washing of feet
he showed us the dignity of service.
Grant that by the power of your Holy Spirit
these signs of our life in faith
may speak again to our hearts,
feed our spirits, and refresh our bodies. Amen.

Good Friday

Thematic

We veil our faces before your glory,
O Holy and Immortal One,
and bow before the cross of your wounded Christ.
With angels and archangels,
we praise you, our Mercy,
and we bless you, our Compassion,
for in our brokenness
you have not abandoned us.
Hear us as we pray through Jesus, our high priest:
heal all division,
reconcile the estranged,
console the suffering,
and raise up to new life
all that is bound by death. Amen.

Intercessory

In this holy time,
as we remember the sacrifice of the cross,
we offer the prayers of our hearts,
that through them we may be transformed
to be servants of justice, love, and peace.

Prayers of the People, concluding with:

Make us steadfast witnesses of our Savior's reign,
that we may live in the pattern of Christ,
who was faithful in all things, even death,
and whose darkest hour gives light and hope. Amen.

Scripture

YEAR A, B, C
Isaiah 52:13—53:12
Psalm 22
Hebrews 10:16-25 *or* Hebrews 4:14-16; 5:7-9
John 18:1—19:42

Grieving God,
on the cross
your Son embraced death
even as he had embraced life:
faithfully and with good courage.
Grant that we who have been
born out of his wounded side
may hold fast to our faith in him exalted
and may find mercy in all times of need. Amen.

Holy Saturday

The following are for use at services other than the Easter Vigil.

Thematic

See the seasonal options on pp. 94–95.

Intercessory

O God, whose face shines upon us,
we offer the prayers we carry deep in our hearts
that those who need deliverance
may know your steadfast love and salvation.

Prayers of the People, concluding with:

Merciful God,
release us from the time of trial and oppression,
that we may witness to the eternal hope
of grief becoming joy
and life rising from death. Amen.

Scripture

YEAR A, B, C
Job 14:1-14 *or* Lamentations 3:1-9, 19-24
Psalm 31:1-4, 15-16
1 Peter 4:1-8
Matthew 27:57-66 *or* John 19:38-42

Eternal God, rock and refuge:
with roots grown old in the earth,
river beds run dry,
and flowers withered in the field,
we wait for revival and release.
Abide with us
until we come alive
in the sunrise of your glory. Amen.

Resurrection of the Lord
Easter Vigil

Thematic

Faithful Midwife,
as you delivered the Hebrews safely
out of the long labor of slavery,
so, morning by morning,
you draw us forth into the new day.
Surround us with a cloud of witnesses,
and sustain us by your powerful word,
that, in the night of loneliness and fear,
we, being weary, may not lose heart
but push toward the joy that is to come,
laboring with Christ
to give birth to your promised kingdom. Amen.

OR

Creator of the universe,
you made the world in beauty,
and restore all things in glory
through the victory of Jesus Christ.
We pray that, wherever your image is still disfigured
by poverty, sickness, selfishness, war, and greed,
the new creation in Jesus Christ may appear in justice, love, and peace,
to the glory of your name. Amen.

OR

Mighty God,
in whom we know the power of redemption,
you stand among us in the shadows of our time.
As we move through every sorrow and trial of this life,
uphold us with knowledge of the final morning
when, in the glorious presence of your risen Son,
we will share in his resurrection,
redeemed and restored to the fullness of life
and forever freed to be your people. Amen.

Intercessory

As we remember the story
of God's gracious presence with us
through life and death,
we lift our prayers on behalf of all creation.

Prayers of the People, concluding with:

God of salvation,
your wisdom and compassion guide us
in the midst of pain and grief,
in the midst of temptation and fear.
Through your resurrection power
heal our sorrow and uplift us in delight,
that we may know the fulfillment of your promise
in our restoration to wholeness. Amen.

Scripture

The following readings and psalms are provided for use at the Easter Vigil. A minimum of three Old Testament readings should be chosen. The reading from Exodus 14 should always be used.

YEAR A, B, C

Old Testament Readings and Psalms
 Genesis 1:1—2:4a
  Psalm 136:1-9, 23-26
 Genesis 7:1-5, 11-18; 8:6-18; 9:8-13
  Psalm 46
 Genesis 22:1-18
  Psalm 16
 Exodus 14:10-31; 15:20-21
  Exodus 15:1b-13, 17-18
 Isaiah 55:1-11
  Isaiah 12:2-6
 Baruch 3:9-15, 32—4:4 *or* Proverbs 8:1-8, 19-21; 9:4b-6
  Psalm 19
 Ezekiel 36:24-28
  Psalm 42 and 43
 Ezekiel 37:1-14
  Psalm 143
 Zephaniah 3:14-20
  Psalm 98

New Testament Reading
 Romans 6:3-11
  Psalm 114

O God of glory,
in the Easter dawn
you raised Jesus from death to life.
As we are united with him in death,
so unite us with him in resurrection,
that we may walk in newness of life. Amen.

Sanctifier of time and space,
maker of dancing quarks and ancient quasars,
of energy and element,
blessed are you, God of gods.
Your saving love endures forever;
your holy light pierces the cold darkness
of death and chaos;
you cut a covenant of life with your creatures,
which no evil can overcome.
May the glorious radiance of resurrection
dispel the shadows in our lives
and conform us more closely to your risen Christ,
to whom, with you and the Holy Spirit,
be all honor, praise, and glory. Amen.

Ever-faithful God,
by divine wisdom you gather us out of the darkness
that has spoken its worst in the death of our Savior,
into the light of Christ.
Enable us to recall your many acts of mercy,
the miracles by which you delivered us,
and the signs of your unwavering love for humankind,
which proclaim the gospel of resurrection and life. Amen.

Resurrection of the Lord
Easter Day

Thematic

Mighty God,
in whom we know the power of redemption,
you stand among us in the shadows of our time.
As we move through every sorrow and trial of this life,
uphold us with knowledge of the final morning
when, in the glorious presence of your risen Son,
we will share in his resurrection,
redeemed and restored to the fullness of life
and forever freed to be your people. Amen.

OR

Living God,
long ago, faithful women
proclaimed the good news
of Jesus' resurrection,
and the world was changed forever.
Teach us to keep faith with them,
that our witness may be as bold,
our love as deep,
and our faith as true. Amen.

OR

Creator of the universe,
you made the world in beauty,
and restore all things in glory
through the victory of Jesus Christ.
We pray that, wherever your image is still disfigured
by poverty, sickness, selfishness, war, and greed,
the new creation in Jesus Christ may appear in justice, love, and peace,
to the glory of your name. Amen.

Intercessory

Let us pray for the needs of the church and the world
to God who raised Jesus to new life.

Prayers of the People, concluding with:

Through the resurrection of your Son, O God,
you destroy the power of death
and remove your people's shame.
By the power of the Spirit,
raise us from sin
and seat us at the paschal feast,
that we may rejoice in the gift of salvation
Jesus has won for us. Amen.

Scripture

YEAR A
Acts 10:34-43 *or* Jeremiah 31:1-6
Psalm 118:1-2, 14-24
Colossians 3:1-4 *or* Acts 10:34-43
John 20:1-18 *or* Matthew 28:1-10

Resurrecting God,
you conquered death
and opened the gates of life everlasting.
In the power of the Holy Spirit,
raise us with Christ
that we, too, may proclaim
healing and peace to the nations. Amen.

YEAR B
Acts 10:34-43 *or* Isaiah 25:6-9
Psalm 118:1-2, 14-24
1 Corinthians 15:1-11 *or* Acts 10:34-43
John 20:1-18 *or* Mark 16:1-8

Love divine,
in raising Christ to new life
you opened the path of salvation to all peoples.
Send us out, with the joy of Mary Magdalene,
to proclaim that we have seen the Lord,
so that all the world may celebrate with you
the banquet of your peace. Amen.

YEAR C

Acts 10:34-43 *or* Isaiah 65:17-25
Psalm 118:1-2, 14-24
1 Corinthians 15:19-26 *or* Acts 10:34-43
John 20:1-18 *or* Luke 24:1-12

We exult in your love,
O God of the living,
for you made the tomb of death
the womb from which you bring forth your Son,
the first-born of a new creation,
and you anointed the universe
with the fragrant Spirit of his resurrection.
Make us joyful witnesses to this good news,
that all humanity may one day
gather at the feast of new life
in the kingdom where you reign
for ever and ever. Amen.

Easter Evening

Thematic

See the prayers for Easter Day, p. 106.

Intercessory

Let us pray for the needs of the church and the world
to God who raised Jesus to new life.

Prayers of the People, concluding with:

Through the resurrection of your Son, O God,
you destroy the power of death
and remove your people's shame.
By the power of the Spirit,
raise us from sin
and seat us at the paschal feast,
that we may rejoice in the gift of salvation
Jesus has won for us. Amen.

Scripture

YEAR A, B, C
Isaiah 25:6-9
Psalm 114
1 Corinthians 5:6b-8
Luke 24:13-49

O God, at this evening hour,
the risen Christ revealed himself to his disciples
in the breaking of bread.
Feed us with the bread of life
and break open our hearts,
that we may know him
not only in the good news of the scriptures,
but risen in the midst of your pilgrim people. Amen.

Easter

Seasonal Prayers

Thematic

Mighty God,
in whom we know the power of redemption,
you stand among us in the shadows of our time.
As we move through every sorrow and trial of this life,
uphold us with knowledge of the final morning
when, in the glorious presence of your risen Son,
we will share in his resurrection,
redeemed and restored to the fullness of life
and forever freed to be your people. Amen.

OR

Living God,
long ago, faithful women
proclaimed the good news
of Jesus' resurrection,
and the world was changed forever.
Teach us to keep faith with them,
that our witness may be as bold,
our love as deep,
and our faith as true. Amen.

OR

Creator of the universe,
you made the world in beauty,
and restore all things in glory
through the victory of Jesus Christ.
We pray that, wherever your image is still disfigured
by poverty, sickness, selfishness, war, and greed,
the new creation in Jesus Christ may appear in justice, love, and peace,
to the glory of your name. Amen.

Intercessory

O God,
your Son remained with his disciples after his resurrection,
teaching them to love all people as neighbors.
As his disciples in this age,
we offer our prayers on behalf of the universe
in which we are privileged to live
and our neighbors with whom we share it.

Prayers of the People, concluding with:

Open our hearts to your power moving
around us and between us and within us,
until your glory is revealed in our love of both friend and enemy,
in communities transformed by justice and compassion,
and in the healing of all that is broken. Amen.

OR

Holy God,
you have called us to follow in the way of your risen Son,
and to care for those who are our companions,
not only with words of comfort, but with acts of love.
Seeking to be true friends of all,
we offer our prayers on behalf of the church and the world.

Prayers of the People, concluding with:

Guide us in the path of discipleship,
so that, as you have blessed us,
we may be a blessing for others,
bringing the promise of the kingdom near
by our words and deeds. Amen.

OR

Sisters and brothers in Christ,
God invites us to bring our doubts and fears,
our joys and concerns, our petitions and praise,
and offer them for the earth and all its creatures.

Prayers of the People, concluding with:

Receive these prayers, O God,
and transform us through them,
that we may have eyes to see and hearts to understand
not only what you do on our behalf,
but what you call us to do
so that your realm will come to fruition in glory. Amen.

Second Sunday of Easter*

Thematic

See the seasonal options on p. 112.

Intercessory

See the seasonal options on p. 113.

Scripture

YEAR A
Acts 2:14a, 22-32
Psalm 16
1 Peter 1:3-9
John 20:19-31

Blessed are you,
O God of our Lord Jesus Christ,
in whom we receive the legacy of a living hope,
born again not only from his death
but also from his resurrection.
May we who have received forgiveness of sins
through the Holy Spirit live to set others free,
until, at length, we enter the inheritance
that is imperishable and unfading,
where Christ lives and reigns with you and the same Spirit. Amen.

YEAR B
Acts 4:32-35
Psalm 133
1 John 1:1—2:2
John 20:19-31

Light of the world,
shine upon us
and disperse the clouds of our selfishness,
that we may reflect the power of the resurrection
in our life together. Amen.

For the Resurrection of the Lord (Easter Vigil, Easter Day, Easter Evening), see pp. 103–109.

Acts 5:27-32
Psalm 118:14-29 *or* Psalm 150
Revelation 1:4-8
John 20:19-31

O God,
you raised up Jesus Christ
as your faithful witness and the first-born of the dead.
By your Holy Spirit, help us to witness to him
so that those who have not yet seen
may come to believe in him
who is, and was, and is to come. Amen.

Third Sunday of Easter

Thematic

See the seasonal options on p. 112.

Intercessory

See the seasonal options on p. 113.

Scripture

YEAR A
Acts 2:14a, 36-41
Psalm 116:1-2, 12-19
1 Peter 1:17-23
Luke 24:13-35

Elusive God,
companion on the way,
you walk behind, beside, beyond;
you catch us unawares.
Break through the disillusionment and despair
clouding our vision,
that, with wide-eyed wonder,
we may find our way
and journey on
as messengers of your good news. Amen.

YEAR B
Acts 3:12-19
Psalm 4
1 John 3:1-7
Luke 24:36b-48

Holy and righteous God,
you raised Christ from the dead
and glorified him at your right hand.
Let the words of scripture,
fulfilled in Jesus your Son,
burn within our hearts
and open our minds to recognize him
in the breaking of bread. Amen.

God of victory over death,
your Son revealed himself again and again,
and convinced his followers of his glorious resurrection.
Grant that we may know his risen presence,
in love obediently feed his sheep,
and care for the lambs of his flock,
until we join the hosts of heaven
in worshiping you and praising him
who is worthy of blessing and honor,
glory and power, for ever and ever. Amen.

Fourth Sunday of Easter

Thematic

See the seasonal options on p. 112.

Intercessory

See the seasonal options on p. 113.

Scripture

YEAR A
Acts 2:42-47
Psalm 23
1 Peter 2:19-25
John 10:1-10

Holy Shepherd,
you know your sheep by name
and lead us to safety through the valleys of death.
Guide us by your voice,
that we may walk in certainty and security
to the joyous feast prepared in your house,
where we celebrate with you forever. Amen.

YEAR B
Acts 4:5-12
Psalm 23
1 John 3:16-24
John 10:11-18

Shepherd of all,
by laying down your life for your flock
you reveal your love for all.
Lead us from the place of death
to the place of abundant life,
that guided by your care for us,
we may rightly offer our lives
in love for you and our neighbors. Amen.

God of comfort and compassion,
through Jesus, your Son, you lead us
to the water of life and the table of your bounty.
May we who have received
the tender love of our Good Shepherd
be strengthened by your grace
to care for your flock. Amen.

Fifth Sunday of Easter

Thematic

See the seasonal options on p. 112.

Intercessory

See the seasonal options on p. 113.

Scripture

YEAR A
Acts 7:55-60
Psalm 31:1-5, 15-16
1 Peter 2:2-10
John 14:1-14

Risen Christ,
you prepare a place for us,
in the home of the Mother-and-Father of us all.
Draw us more deeply into yourself,
through scripture read,
water splashed,
bread broken,
wine poured,
so that when our hearts are troubled,
we will know you more completely
as the way, the truth, and the life. Amen.

YEAR B
Acts 8:26-40
Psalm 22:25-31
1 John 4:7-21
John 15:1-8

God,
you sent your Son into the world
that we might live through him.
May we abide in his risen life
so that we may bear the fruit of love for one another
and know the fullness of joy. Amen.

Alpha and Omega, First and Last,
glory outshining all the lights of heaven:
pour out upon us your Spirit
of faithful love and abundant compassion,
so that we may rejoice in the splendor of your works
while we wait in expectation
for the new heaven and the new earth you promise
when Christ shall come again. Amen.

Sixth Sunday of Easter

Thematic

See the seasonal options on p. 112.

Intercessory

See the seasonal options on p. 113.

Scripture

YEAR A
Acts 17:22-31
Psalm 66:8-20
1 Peter 3:13-22
John 14:15-21

Living and gracious God,
through the death and resurrection of Jesus Christ
you have brought us out to a spacious place
where we are called to live as those redeemed.
Empower us by your Spirit to keep your commandments,
that we may show forth your love
with gentle word and reverent deed
to all your people. Amen.

YEAR B
Acts 10:44-48
Psalm 98
1 John 5:1-6
John 15:9-17

Faithful God,
make our hearts bold with love for one another.
Pour out your Spirit upon all people,
that we may live your justice
and sing in praise
the new song of your marvelous victory. Amen.

Acts 16:9-15
Psalm 67
Revelation 21:10, 22—22:5
John 14:23-29 *or* John 5:1-9

Gracious God,
through a vision you sent forth Paul to preach the gospel
and called the women to the place of prayer on the sabbath.
Grant that we may be sent like Paul
and be found like Lydia,
our hearts responsive to your word
and open to go where you lead us. Amen.

Ascension of the Lord

The following may also be used on the Seventh Sunday of Easter.

Thematic

Risen and ascended Christ,
you surround us with witnesses
and send us the Counselor
who opens our minds to understand your teaching.
Bless us with such grace
that our lives may become a blessing for the world
now, and in the age to come. Amen.

Intercessory

We offer our prayers on behalf
of our neighbors whose needs are known to us.
We pray both for the sisters and brothers we know
and for those who are strangers.

Prayers of the People, concluding with:

Open our minds to understand the scriptures, O God,
so that when sin cripples our hope,
we may discover the freedom of your forgiveness;
when suffering and death overtake our lives,
we may know the joy of the risen Christ;
and when we feel abandoned,
we may comprehend the power of the promised Spirit,
through Jesus Christ our Lord. Amen.

Scripture

Year A, B, C
Acts 1:1-11
Psalm 47 *or* Psalm 93
Ephesians 1:15-23
Luke 24:44-53

Precious Love,
your ascended Son promised the gift of holy power.
Send your Spirit of revelation and wisdom,
that in the blessed freedom of hope,
we may witness to the grace of forgiveness
and sing songs of joy with the peoples of earth
to the One who makes us one body. Amen.

Seventh Sunday of Easter

Thematic/Intercessory

See the seasonal options on pp. 112–113.

Scripture

YEAR A
Acts 1:6-14
Psalm 68:1-10, 32-35
1 Peter 4:12-14; 5:6-11
John 17:1-11

O God of glory,
your Son Jesus Christ suffered for us
and ascended to your right hand.
Unite us with Christ and each other,
in suffering and in joy,
that all your children may be drawn
into your bountiful dwelling. Amen.

YEAR B
Acts 1:15-17, 21-26
Psalm 1
I John 5:9-13
John 17:6-19

Gracious God,
in the resurrection of your Son Jesus Christ,
you have given us eternal life
and glorified your name in all the world.
Refresh our souls with the living streams of your truth,
that in our unity, your joy may be complete. Amen.

YEAR C
Acts 16:16-34
Psalm 97
Revelation 22:12-14, 16-17, 20-21
John 17:20-26

God of boundless grace,
you call us to drink freely of the well of life
and to share the love of your holy being.
May the glory of your love,
made known in the victory of Jesus Christ, our Savior,
transform our lives and the world he lived and died to save.
We ask this in his name and for his sake. Amen.

Day of Pentecost

Thematic

Holy God,
you spoke the world into being.
Pour your Spirit to the ends of the earth,
that your children may return from exile
as citizens of your commonwealth,
and our divisions may be healed
by your word of love and righteousness. Amen.

Intercessory

Empowering God,
you gave the church
the abiding presence of your Holy Spirit.
Look upon your church today and hear our petitions.

Prayers of the People, concluding with:

Grant that, gathered and directed by your Spirit,
we may confess Christ as Lord
and combine our diverse gifts with a singular passion
to continue his mission in this world
until we join in your eternal praise. Amen.

Scripture

If the Old Testament passage (from Numbers in year A, Ezekiel in year B, and Genesis in year C) is chosen for the first reading, the passage from Acts is used as the second reading.

YEAR A
Acts 2:1-21 *or* Numbers 11:24-30
Psalm 104:24-34, 35b
1 Corinthians 12:3b-13 *or* Acts 2:1-21
John 20:19-23 *or* John 7:37-39

Perplexing, Pentecostal God,
you infuse us with your Spirit,
urging us to vision and dream.
May the gift of your presence
find voice in our lives,
that our babbling may be transformed into discernment
and the flickering of many tongues
light an unquenchable fire of compassion and justice. Amen.

Creator Spirit and Giver of life,
make the dry, bleached bones of our lives
live and breathe and grow again
as you did of old.
Pour out your Spirit upon the whole creation.
Come in rushing wind and flashing fire
to turn the sin and sorrow within us
into faith, power, and delight. Amen.

Living God,
you have created all that is.
Send forth your Spirit to renew and restore us,
that we may proclaim your good news
in ways and words
that all will understand and believe. Amen.

Season after
Pentecost

Seasonal Prayers

Thematic Prayers for Series 1

The following thematic prayers, based on the Series 1 semicontinuous first readings of the Revised Common Lectionary in the season after Pentecost, are intended for use by those churches, communions, associations, and denominations where preaching on the Hebrew scriptures is a tradition and where the images of that reading set the theme for worship. The prayers can be used either at the opening of worship to gather the people or as a scripture collect.

YEAR A, Propers 6-13
Abram, Sarai, Isaac, Jacob

To fulfill the ancient promise of salvation, O God,
you made a covenant with our ancestors
and pledged them descendants more numerous than the stars.
Grant that all people may share in the blessings of your covenant,
accomplished through the death and resurrection of your Son
and sealed by the gift of your Spirit. Amen.

OR

Through dreams and visions, O God,
you broaden the horizon and hope of your people,
that they may discover the meaning of your covenant,
even in the midst of trial and exile.
Increase the number of those who believe in your word
so that all people may joyfully respond to your call
and share in your promises. Amen.

YEAR A, Propers 14-15
Joseph

Eternal God,
you are present with us throughout our lives,
even when others plot to do us harm.
May we learn to live together in unity,
that in all we do,
we may sing your praises now and forever. Amen.

God, you are the power of liberation,
calling your servant Moses
to lead your people into freedom,
and giving him the wisdom to proclaim your holy law.
Be our passover from the land of injustice,
be the light that leads us to the perfect rule of love,
that we may be citizens of your unfettered reign;
we ask this through Jesus Christ,
the pioneer of our salvation. Amen.

OR

Through the waters of oppression and death, Lord God,
you led a people into the burning presence of your love.
As you fed them in the desert,
now feed us with the finest of wheat,
that we may know the liberating power of the paschal feast. Amen.

OR

Your voice burns within the depths of our being,
O God of our ancestors,
and draws us into your presence and service.
Hear the cries of your people
and speak a word of comfort,
that we may proclaim to all the earth
the glory of your name. Amen.

OR

On this day of rejoicing, O God of our ancestors,
as we gather to break the bread,
we remember that through the blood of the Lamb
you redeemed us
and made us pass over from death to new life.
Grant that, as we celebrate your mighty deeds,
we may be one with Jesus
in offering you this sacrifice of praise. Amen.

YEAR A, Propers 20-25
Exodus

God of all who wander in the wilderness,
you go before us as beacon and guide.
Lead us through all danger,
sustain us through all desolation,
and bring us home to the land
you have prepared for us. Amen.

YEAR A, Propers 26-28
Promised Land

O Holy God of Israel,
you faithfully keep the promises
you made to our ancestors
and lead your people into the future,
providing hospitality on the way.
Help us who inherit the pilgrim life
to journey faithfully at your command,
that we may be a band of disciples
called to be sojourners in your service. Amen.

OR

God of captives and pilgrims,
you brought your people home from despair
and gave them a land of freedom and plenty.
Look in mercy on us your servants,
deliver us from the prison of selfishness and sin,
and bring us home to justice, sharing, and compassion,
the realm you promised all the world
in Jesus Christ the Savior. Amen.

YEAR B, Propers 4-7
Samuel, Saul, David

Your hand is upon your people, O God,
to guide and protect them through the ages.
Keep in your service
those you have called and anointed,
that the powers of this world may not overwhelm us,
but that, secure in your love,
we may carry out your will
in the face of all adversity. Amen.

OR

O God our ruler and shepherd,
you anointed Jesus
as the king and servant of your people.
Make us attentive to your word,
that we may accept your reign over us
and serve you alone. Amen.

<hr>

YEAR B, Propers 8-14
Reign of David

O God,
sustain us in the complexity of our humanity
as you sustained David—
playing the harp of youth,
throwing stones at giant problems,
loving our friends beyond wisdom,
dancing worship,
mourning children,
breaking our hearts in psalms, and
longing for warmth in our old bones. Amen.

<hr>

YEAR B, Propers 15-16
Solomon

Holy Wisdom,
you granted Solomon's request
for an understanding mind
and the knowledge to discern good from evil.
Fill us with such understanding and knowledge
that we may act as instruments
of your loving desire for creation,
working with you to transform
our conceit into concern for others,
our fear into love,
our violence into peace,
and our brokenness into wholeness. Amen.

YEAR B, Propers 17-20
Wisdom

O God, Wisdom of the universe,
you bear the pain of your people.
Grant us the gift of wisdom,
that we may discern your way
and live justly and graciously
amid the struggles of this world. Amen.

YEAR B, Propers 22-25
Job

Eternal One, whose thoughts and ways are not ours,
you alone are God, awesome, holy, and most high.
School us in the ways of faith and wisdom,
that we, like Job,
may learn to truly see and hear,
and in humility find blessing. Amen.

YEAR B, Propers 26-28
Ruth and Hannah

Providing God,
you journeyed with Ruth
and comforted Hannah
when their lives were burdened by grief.
Grant us faith to believe you will provide a future
where we see none,
that bitterness may turn to joy
and barrenness may bear life. Amen.

YEAR C, Propers 4-9
Elijah and Elisha

Beckoning God,
as you moved in the lives of Elijah and Elisha,
move in our lives,
inviting us to journey to unknown territory,
to listen for your voice,
and to speak your prophetic word
in a world that does not want to hear.
Empowered by your Spirit,
grant us the courage we need
to journey, trust, listen, speak,
and accept your commission
to be your faithful servant people. Amen.

YEAR C, Propers 10-15
Amos, Hosea, Isaiah

God of justice,
your word is light and truth.
Let your face shine on us to restore us,
that we may walk in your way,
seeking justice and doing good. Amen.

YEAR C, Propers 16-24
Jeremiah

God of power and justice,
like Jeremiah you weep over those
who wander from you,
turn aside to other gods,
and enter into chaos and destruction.
By your tears and through your mercy,
teach us your ways
and write them on our hearts
so that we may follow faithfully
the path you show us. Amen.

YEAR C, Propers 25-29
Minor Prophets

God of faithful surprises,
throughout the ages
you have made known your love and power
in unexpected ways and places.
May we daily perceive
the joy and wonder of your abiding presence
and offer our lives in gratitude
for our redemption. Amen.

Intercessory

Friends in Christ,
God invites us to hold the needs of our sisters and brothers
as dear to us as our own needs.
Loving our neighbors as ourselves,
we offer our thanksgivings and our petitions
on behalf of the church and the world.

Prayers of the People, concluding with:

Hear our prayers, God of power,
and through the ministry of your Son
free us from the grip of the tomb,
that we may desire you as the fullness of life
and proclaim your saving deeds to all the world. Amen.

OR

As you heard the prayer of Isaac and Rebekah, O God,
and guided them in the way of your love,
so listen now to those who call upon you.

Prayers of the People, concluding with:

Move us to praise your gracious will,
for in Christ Jesus you have saved us from the deeds of death
and opened for us the hidden ways of your love.
We ask this through Jesus Christ our Lord. Amen.

OR

Lord God, friend of those in need,
your Son Jesus has untied our burdens
and healed our spirits.
We lift up the prayers of our hearts for those still burdened,
those seeking healing,
those in need within the church and the world.

Prayers of the People, concluding with:

Hear our prayers
that we may love you with our whole being
and willingly share the concerns of our neighbors. Amen.

OR

Creator God,
you call us to love and serve you
with body, mind, and spirit
through loving your creation
and our sisters and brothers.
Open our hearts in compassion
and receive these petitions
on behalf of the needs of the church and the world.

Prayers of the People, concluding with:

Holy One,
hear our prayers and make us faithful stewards
of the fragile bounty of this earth
so that we may be entrusted with the riches of heaven. Amen.

OR

We praise your abiding guidance, O God,
for you sent us Jesus, our Teacher and Messiah,
to model for us the way of love for the whole universe.
We offer these prayers of love
on behalf of ourselves and our neighbors,
on behalf of your creation and our fellow creatures.

Prayers of the People, concluding with:

Loving God,
open our ears to hear your word
and draw us closer to you,
that the whole world may be one with you
as you are one with us in Jesus Christ our Lord. Amen.

God of mercy and healing,
you who hear the cries of those in need,
receive these petitions of your people
that all who are troubled
may know peace, comfort, and courage.

Prayers of the People, concluding with:

Life-giving God,
heal our lives,
that we may acknowledge your wonderful deeds
and offer you thanks from generation to generation
through Jesus Christ our Lord. Amen.

OR

God of salvation,
who sent your Son to seek out and save what is lost,
hear our prayers
on behalf of those who are lost in our day,
receiving these petitions and thanksgivings
with your unending compassion.

Prayers of the People, concluding with:

Redeeming Sustainer,
visit your people
and pour out your strength and courage upon us,
that we may hurry to make you welcome
not only in our concern for others,
but by serving them
generously and faithfully in your name. Amen.

Trinity Sunday

First Sunday after Pentecost

Thematic

God of delight,
your Wisdom sings your Word
at the crossroads where humanity and divinity meet.
Invite us into your joyful being
where you know and are known
in each beginning,
in all sustenance,
in every redemption,
that we may manifest your unity
in the diverse ministries you entrust to us,
truly reflecting your triune majesty
in the faith that acts,
in the hope that does not disappoint,
and in the love that endures. Amen.

Intercessory

Holy, holy, holy God,
in calling forth creation from the void,
revealing yourself in human flesh,
and pouring forth your wisdom to guide us,
you manifest your concern for your whole universe.
You invite us, as your people,
to gather the world's needs into our hearts
and bring them before you.

Prayers of the People, concluding with:

Holy, holy, holy God,
fill us with strength and courage,
with discernment and compassion,
that we may be your instruments of justice and love in this world,
that it may be on earth as it is in heaven. Amen.

Scripture

YEAR A
Genesis 1:1—2:4a
Psalm 8
2 Corinthians 13:11-13
Matthew 28:16-20

God, whose fingers sculpt sun and moon
and curl the baby's ear;
Spirit, brooding over chaos
before the naming of day;
Savior, sending us to earth's ends
with water and words:
startle us with the grace, love, and communion
of your unity in diversity,
that we may live to the praise of your majestic name. Amen.

YEAR B
Isaiah 6:1-8
Psalm 29
Romans 8:12-17
John 3:1-17

Holy God,
the earth is full of the glory of your love.
May we your children, born of the Spirit,
so bear witness to your Son Jesus Christ, crucified and risen,
that all the world may believe and have eternal life
through the One who saves,
Father, Son, and Holy Spirit,
now and for ever. Amen.

YEAR C
Proverbs 8:1-4, 22-31
Psalm 8
Romans 5:1-5
John 16:12-15

God of heaven and earth,
before the foundation of the universe and the beginning of time
you are the triune God:
the Author of creation,
the eternal Word of salvation,
and the life-giving Spirit of wisdom.
Guide us to all truth by your Spirit,
that we may proclaim all that Christ revealed
and rejoice in the glory he shared with us.
Glory and praise to you, Father, Son, and Holy Spirit,
now and for ever. Amen.

Proper 4 [9]

Sunday between May 29 and June 4 inclusive*
(if after Trinity Sunday)

Thematic

See the prayers for series 1 on pp. 130–135.

Intercessory

See the seasonal options on pp. 136–138.

Scripture

YEAR A, Series 1
Genesis 6:9-22; 7:24; 8:14-19
Psalm 46
Romans 1:16-17, 3:22b-28 [29-31]
Matthew 7:21-29

God With Us,
whose unfailing mercy is our refuge
even when our broken choices
corrupt your glorious creation:
lead us to the safe haven of righteousness
and uphold us on the rock of your presence,
so that in times of trial
we may stand firm, anchored in faith,
through Christ, our rock and our redeemer. Amen.

YEAR A, Series 2
Deuteronomy 11:18-21, 26-28
Psalm 31:1-5, 19-24
Romans 1:16-17, 3:22b-28 [29-31]
Matthew 7:21-29

In your graciousness, O God of the covenant,
you have revealed the commandments
that open before us a life of blessing and love.
Teach us the wisdom of your law
that we may obey your will
and enter the blessing of the kingdom of heaven.
We ask this through Jesus Christ our Lord. Amen.

*If the Sunday between May 24 and 28 inclusive follows Trinity Sunday, the readings and scripture prayers for the Eighth Sunday after the Epiphany (proper 3) are used on that day.

YEAR B, Series 1
1 Samuel 3:1-10, [11-20]
Psalm 139:1-6, 13-18
2 Corinthians 4:5-12
Mark 2:23—3:6

Holy God,
you search us out
and know us better
than we know ourselves.
As Samuel looked to Eli
for help to discern your voice,
and as the disciples looked to Jesus
for your wisdom on the sabbath,
so raise up in our day faithful servants
who will speak your word to us
with clarity and grace,
with justice and true compassion.
We pray through Christ, the Word made flesh. Amen.

YEAR B, Series 2
Deuteronomy 5:12-15
Psalm 81:1-10
2 Corinthians 4:5-12
Mark 2:23—3:6

Lord of the sabbath, lawgiver and outlaw,
you lift the burdens from our shoulders.
You entrust your treasure to our clay.
Sabbath in us a rest—
joyful as tambourines,
nourishing as bread,
and available to all people, rich and poor—
so that withered bodies and spirits
can be restored. Amen.

YEAR C, Series 1
1 Kings 18:20-21, [22-29], 30-39
Psalm 96
Galatians 1:1-12
Luke 7:1-10

O God, living Lord,
you are the author of faith.
Engrave on our hearts
the gospel revealed in Jesus Christ
and brought near to us by your Holy Spirit,
that we may attest to this faith
in lives that are pleasing to you. Amen.

YEAR C, Series 2
1 Kings 8:22-23, 41-43
Psalm 96:1-9
Galatians 1:1-12
Luke 7:1-10

O Singer, your song is welcome and holiness,
healing and trust.
Teach us a new song to sing your praise,
and tune our ears to melodies we have never heard,
that we may add our voices to the harmony
uniting all creation as one
in adoration and thanksgiving of you,
through Christ, your all-embracing song. Amen.

Proper 5 [10]

*Sunday between June 5 and 11 inclusive
(if after Trinity Sunday)*

Thematic

See the prayers for series 1 on pp. 130–135.

Intercessory

See the seasonal options on pp. 136–138.

Scripture

YEAR A, Series 1
Genesis 12:1-9
Psalm 33:1-12
Romans 4:13-25
Matthew 9:9-13, 18-26

Beckoning God,
you promise long journeys and new names.
Call us out to risk holy adventure
with unusual table companions.
Linger with us
so that we may be faithful disciples,
touching the fringe of your healing
on behalf of all your children. Amen.

YEAR A, Series 2
Hosea 5:15—6:6
Psalm 50:7-15
Romans 4:13-25
Matthew 9:9-13, 18-26

O God,
as the showers renew the earth,
bathe us in your healing power.
Stretch out your hand, that we may live
and know that you alone are God,
in whose faithfulness we have life all our days. Amen.

YEAR B, Series 1
1 Samuel 8:4-11, [12-15], 16-20, [11:14-15]
Psalm 138
2 Corinthians 4:13—5:1
Mark 3:20-35

Unlike earthly kings,
you, O Lord, are ever steadfast and faithful.
You sent us your Son, Jesus the Christ,
to rule over us, not as a tyrant,
but as a gentle shepherd.
Keep us united and strong in faith,
that we may always know your presence in our lives,
and, when you call us home,
may we enter your heavenly kingdom
where you live and reign for ever and ever. Amen.

YEAR B, Series 2
Genesis 3:8-15
Psalm 130
2 Corinthians 4:13—5:1
Mark 3:20-35

God of judgment and mercy,
when we hide ourselves in shame,
you seek us out in love.
Grant us the fullness of your forgiveness,
that as one people, united by your grace,
we may stand with Christ against the powers of evil. Amen.

YEAR C, Series 1
1 Kings 17:8-16 [17-24]
Psalm 146
Galatians 1:11-24
Luke 7:11-17

Provident God,
whose love enfolds the helpless,
the needy, and those who mourn,
give us strength through Jesus Christ
to be instruments of your compassion
to those who are desolate or wounded by life. Amen.

Healing and compassionate God,
your hands hold gently all creation,
your touch brings life in the face of death,
your love transforms destruction into grace.
Touch our lives with your Spirit,
bringing new life and hope,
so that we may live and serve you
with joy and praise. Amen.

OR

Mighty God,
your hands hold the power of life itself.
You restore life in the face of death,
bringing hope out of despair
and promise out of destruction.
Through the breath of your Spirit
bring new life to us,
that we may announce to the world
the power of your presence
made known in Jesus Christ our Savior. Amen.

Proper 6 [11]

Sunday between June 12 and 18 inclusive
(if after Trinity Sunday)

Thematic

See the prayers for series 1 on pp. 130–135.

Intercessory

See the seasonal options on pp. 136–138.

Scripture

YEAR A, Series 1
Genesis 18:1-15, [21:1-7]
Psalm 116:1-2, 12-19
Romans 5:1-8
Matthew 9:35—10:8, [9-23]

God of the prophets and apostles,
you greeted old Abraham and Sarah
with news of wonder and life.
Send us into the world
to preach good news, as Jesus did,
heal the sick,
resist evil,
and bring the outcast home. Amen.

YEAR A, Series 2
Exodus 19:2-8a
Psalm 100
Romans 5:1-8
Matthew 9:35—10:8, [9-23]

God of compassion,
you have opened the way for us
and brought us to yourself.
Pour your love into our hearts,
that, overflowing with joy,
we may freely share the blessings of your realm
and faithfully proclaim the good news of Christ. Amen.

1 Samuel 15:34—16:13
Psalm 20
2 Corinthians 5:6-10, [11-13], 14-17
Mark 4:26-34

Mighty God,
to you belong the mysteries of the universe.
You transform shepherds into kings,
the smallest seeds into magnificent trees,
and hardened hearts into loving ones.
Bless us with your life-giving Spirit,
re-create us in your image,
and shape us to your purposes,
through Jesus Christ. Amen.

YEAR B, Series 2

Ezekiel 17:22-24
Psalm 92:1-4, 12-15
2 Corinthians 5:6-10, [11-13], 14-17
Mark 4:26-34

Creating God,
your reign of love makes all things new.
Plant seeds of confidence and gladness in our hearts,
so that, trusting your word,
we may live no longer for ourselves
but for him who died and was raised for us,
Jesus Christ our Lord. Amen.

YEAR C, Series 1

1 Kings 21:1-10, [11-14], 15-21a
Psalm 5:1-8
Galatians 2:15-21
Luke 7:36—8:3

God of compassion,
you suffer in the grief of your people,
and you are present to heal and forgive.
May the sun of your justice rise on every night of oppression,
and may the warm rays of your healing love
renew each troubled mind;
for you are the God of salvation and new life,
made known to us in Jesus Christ our Lord. Amen.

Merciful God,
your ready forgiveness makes us bold to confess our sins.
Grant that we may die to sin
and become fully alive by faith in Jesus Christ,
who lives and reigns with you
in the unity of the Holy Spirit. Amen.

Proper 7 [12]

*Sunday between June 19 and June 25 inclusive
(if after Trinity Sunday)*

Thematic

See the prayers for series 1 on pp. 130–135.

Intercessory

See the seasonal options on pp. 136–138.

Scripture

YEAR A, Series 1
Genesis 21:8-21
Psalms 86:1-10, 16-17
Romans 6:1b-11
Matthew 10:24-39

God of strength and courage,
in Jesus Christ you set us free from sin and death,
and call us to the risk of faith and service.
Give us grace to follow him
who gave himself for others,
that, by our service,
we may find the life he came to bring. Amen.

YEAR A, Series 2
Jeremiah 20:7-13
Psalm 67:7-10, [11-15], 16-18
Romans 6:1b-11
Matthew 10:24-39

God of power,
you uphold us in times of persecution
and strengthen us to meet the trials of faithful witness.
As you delivered us from death
through our baptism in Christ
and the victory of his resurrection,
send us forth to proclaim that glorious redemption,
so that the world may claim
the freedom of forgiveness
and new life in you. Amen.

YEAR B, Series 1
1 Samuel 17:[1a, 4-11, 19-23], 32-49
Psalm 9:9-20
  or 1 Samuel 17:57—18:5, 10-16
  Psalm 133
2 Corinthians 6:1-13
Mark 4:35-41

God our protector,
you stood by David in the time of trial.
Stand with us through all life's storms,
giving us courage to risk danger
to protect those who are oppressed and poor,
that they may know you
as their stronghold and hope. Amen.

YEAR B, Series 2
Job 38:1-11
Psalm 107:1-3, 23-32
2 Corinthians 6:1-13
Mark 4:35-41

Keeper of our lives,
you know the hardness and gentleness of human hearts.
You call your people to faithful living.
Through the storms of life
that bring suffering and fear, joy and laughter,
teach us to turn to you for all we need,
so that we may come to know your presence
even in the midst of the trials that surround us. Amen.

YEAR C, Series 1
1 Kings 19:1-4 [5-7] 8-15a
Psalms 42 and 43
Galatians 3:23-29
Luke 8:26-39

God our refuge and hope,
when race, status, or gender divide us,
when despondency and despair haunt and afflict us,
when community lies shattered:
comfort and convict us with the stillness of your presence,
that we may confess all you have done,
through Christ to whom we belong
and in whom we are one. Amen.

YEAR C, Series 2
Isaiah 65:1-9
Psalm 22:19-28
Galatians 3:23-29
Luke 8:26-39

Most holy and eternal God,
you dwell in the heights of heaven,
yet you walk among those who refuse to see you.
Hold out your hand to those who rebel against you,
and free us from the chains that bind us,
that we may be healed by Christ
and proclaim his saving deeds to all the world. Amen.

Proper 8 [13]

Sunday between June 26 and July 2 inclusive

Thematic

See the prayers for series 1 on pp. 130–135.

Intercessory

See the seasonal options on pp. 136–138.

Scripture

YEAR A, Series 1
Genesis 22:1-14
Psalm 13
Romans 6:12-23
Matthew 10:40-42

Ruler of the universe,
you call us to radical loyalty
beyond all earthly claim.
Grant us strength to offer ourselves to you
as people who have been raised from death to life
through Jesus Christ,
who lives and reigns with you and the Holy Spirit,
one God, now and for ever. Amen.

YEAR A, Series 2
Jeremiah 28:5-9
Psalm 89:1-4, 15-18
Romans 6:12-23
Matthew 10:40-42

Faithful God,
your love stands firm from generation to generation,
your mercy is always abundant.
Give us open and understanding hearts,
that having heard your word,
we may seek Christ's presence in all whom we meet. Amen.

YEAR B, Series 1
2 Samuel 1:1, 17-27
Psalm 130
2 Corinthians 8:7-15
Mark 5:21-43

God of hope,
you are ruler of night as well as day,
guardian of those who wander in the shadows.
Be new light and life
for those who live in the darkness of despair,
for prisoners of guilt and grief,
for victims of fantasy and depression,
that even where death's cold grip tightens,
we may know the power of the one
who conquered fear and death. Amen.

YEAR B, Series 2
Wisdom of Solomon 1:13-15; 2:23-24 or Lamentations 3:22-33
Psalm 30
2 Corinthians 8:7-15
Mark 5:21-43

Companion in life and death,
your love is steadfast and never ends;
our weeping may linger with night,
but you give joy in the morning.
Touch us with your healing grace
that, restored to wholeness,
we may live out our calling
as your resurrection people. Amen.

YEAR C, Series 1
2 Kings 2:1-2, 6-14
Psalm 77:1-2, 11-20
Galatians 5:1, 13-25
Luke 9:51-62

O God, you set us free in Jesus Christ
with a power greater than all that would keep us captive.
Grant that we might live gracefully in our freedom
without selfishness or arrogance,
and through love become slaves
to the freedom of the gospel
for the sake of your reign. Amen.

God, you call us to go where Christ leads.
Turn us from the ways of the world;
guide us to fullness of joy in the Spirit,
where bodies and souls rest secure;
and grant us strength
to follow the way of the cross,
which frees us to love one another
for the sake of all creation. Amen.

Proper 9 [14]

Sunday between July 3 and 9 inclusive

Thematic

See the prayers for series 1 on pp. 130–135.

Intercessory

See the seasonal options on pp. 136–138.

Scripture

YEAR A, Series 1

Genesis 24:34-38, 42-49, 58-67
Psalm 45:10-17 *or* Song of Solomon 2:8-13
Romans 7:15-25a
Matthew 11:16-19, 25-30

We give you thanks, O God of compassion,
for the salvation you have revealed to the little ones
through Christ Jesus, our wisdom and strength.
Teach us to take up his gentle yoke
and find rest from our burdens and cares. Amen.

YEAR A, Series 2

Zechariah 9:9-12
Psalm 145:8-14
Romans 7:15-25a
Matthew 11:16-19, 25-30

We rejoice, O Christ,
for in your tender compassion
you shoulder our burdens and ease our heavy hearts.
Give us the strength to carry each other
as you have carried us. Amen.

YEAR B, Series 1
2 Samuel 5:1-5, 9-10
Psalm 48
2 Corinthians 12:2-10
Mark 6:1-13

Guardian of the weak,
through the teachings of your prophets
you have claimed our cities, towns, and homes
as temples of your presence and citadels of your justice.
Turn the places we live into strongholds of your grace,
that the most vulnerable
as well as the most powerful among us
may find peace in the security
that comes in the strong name of Jesus Christ. Amen.

YEAR B, Series 2
Ezekiel 2:1-5
Psalm 123
2 Corinthians 12:2-10
Mark 6:1-13

God of grace and powerful weakness,
at times your prophets were ignored, rejected, belittled, and unwelcome.
Trusting that we, too, are called to be prophets,
fill us with your Spirit,
and support us by your gentle hands,
that we may persevere in speaking your word
and living our faith. Amen.

YEAR C, Series 1
2 Kings 5:1-14
Psalm 30
Galatians 6:[1-6], 7-16
Luke 10:1-11, 16-20

God of fresh beginnings,
you make all things new
in the wisdom of Jesus Christ.
Make us agents of your transforming power
and heralds of your reign of justice and peace,
that all may share in the healing Christ brings. Amen.

God of all nations and peoples,
your Son commanded his disciples
to preach and heal throughout the world.
Grant us, by the power of the Holy Spirit,
the zeal to proclaim the good news of peace and justice,
and gather all humanity into life with you. Amen.

Proper 10 [15]

Sunday between July 10 and 16 inclusive

Thematic

See the prayers for series 1 on pp. 130–135.

Intercessory

See the seasonal options on pp. 136–138.

Scripture

YEAR A, Series 1
Genesis 25:19-34
Psalm 119:105-112
Romans 8:1-11
Matthew 13:1-9, 18-23

O God of mercy,
in Jesus Christ you freed us from sin and death,
and by your Holy Spirit
you nourish our mortal bodies with life.
Plant us now in good soil,
that our lives may flower
in righteousness and peace. Amen.

YEAR A, Series 2
Isaiah 55:10-13
Psalm 65:[1-8], 9-13
Romans 8:1-11
Matthew 13:1-9, 18-23

Ancient Gardener,
your holy word is planted in our hearts
as good seed in fertile soil.
So nurture us
that we may bear fruit abundantly. Amen.

2 Samuel 6:1-5, 12b-19
Psalm 24
Ephesians 1:3-14
Mark 6:14-29

God of hosts, before whom David danced and sang,
Mother of mercy and Father of our Lord Jesus Christ,
in whom all things cohere:
whenever we are confronted by
lust, hate, or fear,
give us the faith of John the baptizer,
that we may trust in the redemption of your Messiah. Amen.

YEAR B, Series 2
Amos 7:7-15
Psalm 85:8-13
Ephesians 1:3-14
Mark 6:14-29

Steadfast God,
your prophets set the plumb line
of your righteousness and truth
in the midst of your people.
Grant us the courage
to judge ourselves against it.
Straighten all that is crooked or warped within us
until our hearts and souls stretch upright,
blameless and holy,
to meet the glory of Christ. Amen.

YEAR C, Series 1
Amos 7:7-17
Psalm 82
Colossians 1:1-14
Luke 10:25-37

Divine Judge,
you framed the earth with love and mercy
and declared it good;
yet we, desiring to justify ourselves,
judge others harshly,
without knowledge or understanding.
Keep us faithful in prayer
that we may be filled with the knowledge of your will,
and not ignore or pass by another's need,
but plumb the depths of love in showing mercy. Amen.

Almighty God,
you give the holy law to your people
so that it will always be near us and our children.
Through our Lord Jesus who has fulfilled the law in every way,
grant that we may love you with heart, soul, strength, and mind,
and our neighbor as ourselves. Amen.

Proper 11 [16]

Sunday between July 17 and 23 inclusive

Thematic

See the prayers for series 1 on pp. 130–135.

Intercessory

See the seasonal options on pp. 136–138.

Scripture

YEAR A, Series 1
Genesis 28:10-19a
Psalm 139:1-12, 23-24
Romans 8:12-25
Matthew 13:24-30, 36-43

O God of Jacob,
you speak in the light of day
and in the dark of night
when our sleeping is filled with dreams of heaven and earth.
May Jacob's vision
remind us to be open and watchful,
ready to discover your presence in our midst. Amen.

YEAR A, Series 2
Wisdom of Solomon 12:13, 16-19 or Isaiah 44:6-8
Psalm 86:11-17
Romans 8:12-25
Matthew 13:24-30, 36-43

Faithful God,
you care for us with compassion and firmness,
urging us to grow in love for you.
Through Christ,
may we hear more deeply
your call to be rooted in your way. Amen.

OR

Steadfast God,
teach us your way and your truth.
Root us in you alone,
help us to grow in grace and love,
that we may fulfill our role and our work
in the reign of Jesus Christ. Amen.

Holy God of Israel,
ever present and moving among your people,
draw us near to you,
that in place of hostility there may be peace;
in place of loneliness, compassion;
in place of aimlessness, direction;
and in place of sickness, healing;
through Christ Jesus, in whom you draw near to us. Amen.

Shepherd God,
your call us into a rhythm of work and rest
that our lives may be the better for it.
So shape our leisure and our labor,
that the world will recognize us
as Jesus' disciples
and our ministry
as what you would have us do. Amen.

Ever-faithful God,
whose being is perfect righteousness:
reconcile us in your Son
with the helpless and the needy,
with those we would ignore or oppress,
and with those we have called enemies,
that we may serve all people as your hands of love,
and sit at the feet of those
who need our compassionate care. Amen.

O God of Abraham and Sarah,

in due season, you fulfilled a promise almost too wonderful to imagine.

Awaken us to the workings of your will in our midst,

and keep us attentive to the things that matter,

until the day when your mystery,

hidden throughout the ages,

stands fully revealed in the kingdom of all your saints. Amen.

Proper 12 [17]

Sunday between July 24 and 30 inclusive

Thematic

See the prayers for series 1 on pp. 130–135.

Intercessory

See the seasonal options on pp. 136–138.

Scripture

YEAR A, Series 1
Genesis 29:15-28
Psalm 105:1-11, 45b *or* Psalm 128
Romans 8:26-39
Matthew 13:31-33, 44-52

Seed-planting, fish-netting, bread-baking, pearl-hunting God,
you shape us into living parables.
Pray with your Spirit in us
so that we may understand our experiences
as healing metaphors,
and become creative and abundant stewards
of the environment you entrusted to our love. Amen.

YEAR A, Series 2
I Kings 3:5-12
Psalm 119:129-136
Romans 8:26-39
Matthew 13:31-33, 44-52

O sovereign God,
in Jesus Christ you set your holy reign upon this earth
and within your people.
So let its coming
be like the mustard seed
that grows into greatness,
and like the leaven
that mixes with the grain
until the whole becomes greater,
to the praise of the triune God,
who lives forevermore. Amen.

In your compassionate love, O God,
you nourish us with the words of life and bread of blessing.
Grant that Jesus may calm our fears
and move our hearts to praise your goodness
by sharing our bread with others. Amen.

Sustainer of the hungry,
like a mother you long to feed your children
until each is satisfied.
Turn our eyes to you alone,
that, aware of our own deepest longings,
we will reach out with Christ
to feed others with the miracle of your love. Amen.

Living God, you raise us to fullness of being
in sharing the Christ-life together.
Teach us to pray
and grant us hopeful persistence
in seeking your will and your way,
that by the power of the Spirit,
love and faithfulness may meet
to disarm the powers of the world. Amen.

YEAR C, Series 2
Genesis 18:20-32
Psalm 138
Colossians 2:6-15, [16-19]
Luke 11:1-13

Father in heaven,
in your goodness
you pour out on your people all that they need,
and satisfy those who persist in prayer.
Make us bold in asking,
thankful in receiving,
tireless in seeking,
and joyful in finding,
that we may always proclaim your coming kingdom
and do your will on earth as in heaven. Amen.

Proper 13 [18]

Sunday between July 31 and August 6 inclusive

Thematic

See the prayers for series 1 on pp. 130–135.

Intercessory

See the seasonal options on pp. 136–138.

Scripture

YEAR A, Series 1
Genesis 32:22-31
Psalm 17:1-7, 15
Romans 9:1-5
Matthew 14:13-21

God beyond all seeing and knowing,
we meet you in the night of change and crisis,
and wrestle with you in the darkness of doubt.
Give us the will and spirit
to live faithfully and love as we are loved. Amen.

YEAR A, Series 2
Isaiah 55:1-5
Psalm 145:8-9, 14-21
Romans 9:1-5
Matthew 14:13-21

Glorious God,
your generosity floods the world with goodness
and you shower creation with abundance.
Awaken in us a hunger for food
to satisfy both body and heart,
that in the miracle of being fed
we may be empowered to feed the hungry in Jesus' name. Amen.

YEAR B, Series 1
2 Samuel 11:26—12:13a
Psalm 51:1-12
Ephesians 4:1-16
John 6:24-35

God of the lowly and the mighty,
you know the ugliness of your people
when we harm and destroy one another,
yet you offer us
forgiveness of our sins if we but turn to you.
Expand our hearts to receive the mercy you give us,
that, in turn, we may share your grace and mercy
with others each moment of our lives. Amen

YEAR B, Series 2
Exodus 16:2-4, 9-15
Psalm 78:23-29
Ephesians 4:1-16
John 6:24-35

God of hope,
when your hungry people longed for the slave food of Egypt,
you opened the doors of heaven and rained down manna.
Feed us with the bread of life at your table,
that we may taste the freedom of eternal life
and lead lives worthy of our calling,
through Christ our head. Amen.

YEAR C, Series 1
Hosea 11:1-11
Psalm 107:1-9, 43
Colossians 3:1-11
Luke 12:13-21

Generous God,
in abundance you give us things both spiritual and physical.
Help us to hold lightly the fading things of this earth
and grasp tightly the lasting things of your kingdom,
so that what we are and do and say
may be our gifts to you
through Christ, who beckons all to seek the things above,
where he lives and reigns with you and the Holy Spirit. Amen.

Generous Giver,
you pour forth your extravagant bounty without measure
upon your whole creation.
Teach us such generosity,
that the fruits of our spirits
and the works of our hands may be used
for the building of your commonwealth of blessing. Amen.

Proper 14 [19]

Sunday between August 7 and 13 inclusive

Thematic

See the prayers for series 1 on pp. 130–135.

Intercessory

See the seasonal options on pp. 136–138.

Scripture

YEAR A, Series 1
Genesis 37:1-4, 12-28
Psalm 105:1-6, 16-22, 45b
Romans 10:5-15
Matthew 14:22-33

Through the storms of life, O God,
you are with your people
in the person of Jesus your Son.
Calm our fears and strengthen our faith
that we may never doubt his presence among us
but proclaim that he is your Son,
risen from the dead,
living for ever and ever. Amen.

YEAR A, Series 2
I Kings 19:9-18
Psalm 85:8-13
Romans 10:5-15
Matthew 14:22-33

God of awe, from whom we flee in holy terror:
your silence burns like ice;
your whisper cuts through fear;
we long to hear your faithful word
of righteousness and peace.
Bless us with bold belief
even in the darkness of the night
and the assault of life's storms,
that we may be messengers of your justice,
in the name of the One whom wind and wave obey. Amen.

YEAR B, Series 1
2 Samuel 18:5-9, 15, 31-33
Psalm 130
Ephesians 4:25—5:2
John 6:35, 41-51

Bread of heaven, you feed us in the depths
of grief, sin, and hostility.
Nourish us with your word
through the long hours of tears,
and in the dawning awareness
of our need for forgiveness,
so that we may be redeemed by your steadfast love. Amen.

YEAR B, Series 2
1 Kings 19:4-8
Psalm 34:1-8
Ephesians 4:25—5:2
John 6:35, 41-51

Bread of life,
you taught us to put away bitterness and anger,
and with tenderhearted kindness
to share the fruit of our labor with the needy.
Strengthen us by your grace,
that in communion with you,
we may forgive one another
and live in love as Christ loved us. Amen.

YEAR C, Series 1
Isaiah 1:1, 10-20
Psalm 50:1-8, 22-23
Hebrews 11:1-3, 8-16
Luke 12:32-40

God of judgment and grace,
you ask not for sacrifices,
but lives of trusting faith
that acknowledge your power and mercy.
Give us faith as deep and strong as Abraham's and Sarah's,
that we may follow you through all our days
as did Jesus Christ our Savior. Amen.

God of Abraham and Jesus,
you invite your people
to contemplate heavenly things
and urge us toward faith in you.
May your coming among us
find our doors open,
our tables set,
and all your people ready to greet you. Amen.

Proper 15 [20]

Sunday between August 14 and 20 inclusive

Thematic

See the prayers for series 1 on pp. 130–135.

Intercessory

See the seasonal options on pp. 136–138.

Scripture

YEAR A, Series 1
Genesis 45:1-15
Psalm 133
Romans 11:1-2a, 29-32
Matthew 15:[10-20], 21-28

Holy One of Israel, covenant-keeper,
you restore what is lost,
heal what is wounded,
and gather in those who have been rejected.
Give us the faith
to speak as steadfastly as did the Canaanite woman,
that the outcast may be welcomed
and all people may be blessed. Amen.

YEAR A, Series 2
Isaiah 56:1, 6-8
Psalm 67
Romans 11:1-2a, 29-32
Matthew 15:[10-20], 21-28

God of the foreigner and outcast,
your arms reach out to embrace
all those who call upon you.
Teach us as disciples of Christ
so to love the world
that your name may be known
throughout the earth. Amen.

1 Kings 2:10-12; 3:3-14
Psalm 111
Ephesians 5:15-20
John 6:51-58

Living God,
you are the giver of wisdom and true discernment,
guiding those who seek your ways to choose the good.
Mercifully grant that your people,
feasting on the true bread of heaven,
may have eternal life in Jesus Christ our Lord. Amen.

YEAR B, Series 2
Proverbs 9:1-6
Psalm 34:9-14
Ephesians 5:15-20
John 6:51-58

Holy Wisdom, God of abundant life,
you call us to the banquet of your love.
We find you in the gifts you give;
we know you in the ones with whom we share this holy food,
and in the bread of this table, your Son, Jesus Christ.
Grant that we may be bread for others,
as he is bread for us. Amen.

YEAR C, Series 1
Isaiah 5:1-7
Psalm 80:1-2, 8-19
Hebrews 11:29—12:2
Luke 12:49-56

Judge eternal,
you love justice and hate oppression;
you give peace to those who seek it,
and you condemn the rage of violence.
Give us courage to take our stand
with all victims of bloodshed and greed,
and, following your servants and prophets,
look to Jesus, the pioneer and perfecter of our faith. Amen.

YEAR C, Series 2
Jeremiah 22:23-29
Psalm 82
Hebrews 11:29—12:2
Luke 12:49-56

God of all the nations,
you rescued your people out of the Red Sea
and delivered Rahab from battle;
you rescue the lowly and needy from injustice and tribulation.
Surround us with so great a cloud of witnesses
that we may have faith to live by your word in our time,
courage to persevere in the race set before us,
and endurance in the time of trial. Amen.

Proper 16 [21]

Sunday between August 21 and 27 inclusive

Thematic

See the prayers for series 1 on pp. 130–135.

Intercessory

See the seasonal options on pp. 136–138.

Scripture

YEAR A, Series 1
Exodus 1:8—2:10
Psalm 124
Romans 12:1-8
Matthew 16:13-20

God of Miriam and Moses,
you are our help from age to age.
Accept our worship, our living sacrifice,
and transform us by your Spirit,
that, being many members of one true body,
we may dare to pray together
in the name of Christ the Lord. Amen.

YEAR A, Series 2
Isaiah 51:1-6
Psalm 138
Romans 12:1-8
Matthew 16:13-20

O God,
you blessed Abraham and Sarah,
and made them a great nation.
Keep us in remembrance
of the rock from which we are hewn,
that the waste places of our lives
may blossom to your glory. Amen.

Gracious God,
although we once were strangers,
you receive us as friends
and draw us home to you.
Set your living bread before us
that, feasting around your table,
we may be strengthened to continue the work
to which your Son commissioned us. Amen.

Source of life,
you feed us with the spiritual milk of your love
and deliver us from darkness to light.
Encompass us in the circle of your protection,
that, secure in your sustaining power,
we may find the wisdom and strength
to challenge the evils of our time. Amen.

Living God, you formed us in the womb
and appointed us to be prophets to the nations.
Stretch out your hand to cure our infirmity
and dispel our fear,
that we may know the freedom of serving you in Christ
and proclaim the wonders you have done. Amen.

YEAR C, Series 2
Isaiah 58:9b-14
Psalm 103:1-8
Hebrews 12:18-29
Luke 13:10-17

Merciful God,
as we pour out the wealth you have entrusted to us,
the parched places are watered;
as we cease our evil talk,
the rising light of peace dawns in the darkness.
So lead us into faithful living
that your promises may unfold in us
as a woman's back, long bent, unfolds at Christ's command,
to the praise of your holy name. Amen.

Proper 17 [22]

Sunday between August 28 and September 3 inclusive

Thematic

See the prayers for series 1 on pp. 130–135.

Intercessory

See the seasonal options on pp. 136–138.

Scripture

YEAR A, Series 1
Exodus 3:1-15
Psalm 105:1-6, 23-26, 45b
Romans 12:9-21
Matthew 16:21-28

In the flaming bush
you promised deliverance to your people, O God,
and in the cross of Jesus
you embraced our suffering and pain.
In times of misery,
show us the transforming power of your love
that we may know the hope of your glory. Amen.

YEAR A, Series 2
Jeremiah 15:15-21
Psalm 26:1-8
Romans 12:9-21
Matthew 16:21-28

Faithful God,
you are the hope of all the oppressed,
and the source of freedom for those held captive.
Make us strong to witness to your liberating power,
in generosity of life and in humility of spirit,
that all the world may delight in your goodness. Amen.

YEAR B, Series 1
Song of Solomon 2:8-13
Psalm 45:1-2, 6-9
James 1:17-27
Mark 7:1-8, 14-15, 21-23

Blessed are you, O Lord and Lover,
source of beauty and depth of passion.
Strengthen and inspire us to do the word we hear
and live the faith we confess. Amen.

YEAR B, Series 2
Deuteronomy 4:1-2, 6-9
Psalm 15
James 1:17-27
Mark 7:1-8, 14-15, 21-23

O Father of lights,
from whose word of truth
we have been born as firstfruits of your creatures:
make us quick to listen and slow to speak,
that the word implanted in us
may take root to nourish all our living,
and that we may be blessed in our doing
and fruitful in action. Amen.

YEAR C, Series 1
Jeremiah 2:4-13
Psalm 81:1, 10-16
Hebrews 13:1-8, 15-16
Luke 14:1, 7-14

God of majestic glory,
in humility you have revealed yourself
in the incarnation of your Son, Jesus Christ,
who took the lowest place among us
that we might be raised to the heights of divinity.
Teach us to walk the path he prepared for us,
so that we might take a place at the table
with all who seek the joy of his kingdom. Amen.

Almighty God,
in your goodness, you provide for the needy.
Remove from your people the pride of place
and the pursuit of power that mocks humility.
Open our hearts in generosity and justice
to the neglected and lonely,
that in showing esteem for others,
we may honor and please you
through Jesus Christ in the Holy Spirit. Amen.

Proper 18 [23]

Sunday between September 4 and 10 inclusive

Thematic

See the prayers for series 1 on pp. 130–135.

Intercessory

See the seasonal options on pp. 136–138.

Scripture

YEAR A, Series 1
Exodus 12:1-14
Psalm 149
Romans 13:8-14
Matthew 18:15-20

Holy God,
you call us to righteousness and light.
Teach us the undivided law of love,
that we may love your children even as you do,
love you with all our will and strength,
and find our freedom in this blessed service,
taught to us in word and deed
by Jesus Christ our Lord. Amen.

YEAR A, Series 2
Ezekiel 33:7-11
Psalm 119:33-40
Romans 13:8-14
Matthew 18:15-20

God among us,
we gather in the name of your Son
to learn love for one another.
Turn our feet from evil paths,
our hands from shameful deeds,
our minds to your wisdom,
and our hearts to your grace. Amen.

Holy Lord, maker of us all,
you call us to love our neighbors as ourselves
and teach us that faith without works is dead.
Open us to the opportunities for ministry that lie before us,
where faith and works and the need of our neighbor
come together in the name of Jesus Christ, our Savior. Amen.

YEAR B, Series 2
Isaiah 35:4-7a
Psalm 146
James 2:1-10, [11-13], 14-17
Mark 7:24-37

God, whose love streams like fresh water
into the deserts of our hearts,
you turn us from greed and partiality
to healing and justice.
Make us companions of those who long for your deliverance,
and give us safe passage at the last
into the land of your shalom. Amen.

YEAR C, Series 1
Jeremiah 18:1-11
Psalm 139:1-6, 13-18
Philemon 1-21
Luke 14:25-33

Creator God,
you form us on the wheel of life
as a potter molds the clay.
Shape us into holy vessels,
bearing the mark of your wise crafting,
that we may remain strong and useful
through years of faithful and obedient service
in Christ's name. Amen.

Source of life and blessing,
of garden, orchard, field,
root us in obedience to you
and nourish us by your ever-flowing Spirit,
that, perceiving only the good we might do,
our lives may be fruitful,
our labor productive,
and our service useful,
in communion with Jesus, our brother. Amen.

Proper 19 [24]

Sunday between September 11 and 17 inclusive

Thematic

See the prayers for series 1 on pp. 130–135.

Intercessory

See the seasonal options on pp. 136–138.

Scripture

YEAR A, Series 1
Exodus 14:19-31
Psalm 114 *or* Exodus 15:1b-11, 20-21
Romans 14:1-12
Matthew 18:21-35

God of freedom,
you brought your people out of slavery with a mighty hand.
Deliver us from our captivity to pride
and indifference to the needs and gifts of others,
that we may be ready to love as you have loved us,
and to give even as we have received. Amen.

YEAR A, Series 2
Genesis 50:15-21
Psalm 103:[1-7], 8-13
Romans 14:1-12
Matthew 18:21-35

O God of Joseph and all his brothers,
your forgiveness transcends
whatever wrong exists between us.
Grant us the courage to forgive others,
and to practice reconciliation
by the kindness of our speaking,
the sharing of our resources,
and the honoring of your desire for good. Amen.

YEAR B, Series 1
Proverbs 1:20-33
Psalm 19 *or* Wisdom of Solomon 7:26—8:1
James 3:1-12
Mark 8:27-38

Wisdom of God,
from the street corners and at the entrances to the city
you proclaim the way of life and of death.
Grant us the wisdom to recognize your Messiah,
that following in the way of the cross,
we may know the way of life and glory. Amen.

YEAR B, Series 2
Isaiah 50:4-9a
Psalm 116:1-9
James 3:1-12
Mark 8:27-38

Through suffering and rejection, O God,
you bring forth our salvation,
for in Jesus you embrace our humanity
and transform our lives by the glory of his cross.
Grant that for the sake of the gospel
we may rebuke the lure of this world,
take up our cross,
and follow your Son Jesus Christ. Amen.

YEAR C, Series 1
Jeremiah 4:11-12, 22-28
Psalm 14
1 Timothy 1:12-17
Luke 15:1-10

Merciful God,
your desire to bring us into your commonwealth
is so great that you seek us
in the places of our ignorance,
and the forgotten corners where we hide in despair.
Gather us into your loving embrace,
and pour upon us your wise and holy Spirit,
so that we may become faithful servants
in whom you rejoice with all the company of heaven. Amen.

Persistently forgiving God,
we are a stiff-necked and stubborn people
who try your patience;
yet, instead of giving us up for lost,
you seek us out until we return to you.
Break our willfulness
and bring us back from our wanderings;
bend our pride
and create in us pure and faithful hearts,
which rejoice in your forgiveness
made known through Jesus Christ. Amen.

Proper 20 [25]

Sunday between September 18 and 24 inclusive

Thematic

See the prayers for series 1 on pp. 130–135.

Intercessory

See the seasonal options on pp. 136–138.

Scripture

YEAR A, Series 1
Exodus 16:2-15
Psalm 105:1-6, 37-45
Philippians 1:21-30
Matthew 20:1-16

O God,
from your providing hand even the dissatisfied and grumbling
receive what they need for their lives.
Teach us your ways of justice
and lead us to practice your generosity,
so that we may live a life worthy of the gospel
made known through your Son Jesus Christ, our Savior. Amen.

YEAR A, Series 2
Jonah 3:10—4:11
Psalm 145:1-8
Philippians 1:21-30
Matthew 20:1-16

God of miracles and of mercy,
all creation sings your praise.
Like the vineyard owner,
your grace is extravagant and unexpected.
Lead us to repentance
and the acceptance of your grace,
that we may witness to your love,
which embraces both those we call friend
and those we call stranger. Amen.

Proverbs 31:10-31
Psalm 1
James 3:13—4:3, 7-8a
Mark 9:30-37

God of unsearchable mystery and light,
your weakness is greater than our strength,
your foolishness brings all our cleverness to naught,
your gentleness confounds the power we would claim.
You call first to be last and last to be first,
servant to be leader and ruler to be underling of all.
Pour into our hearts the wisdom of your Word and Spirit,
that we may know your purpose and live to your glory. Amen.

Wisdom of Solomon 1:16—2:1, 12-22 *or* Jeremiah 11:18-20
Psalm 54
James 3:13—4:3, 7-8a
Mark 9:30-37

O God, our teacher and guide,
you draw us to yourself
and welcome us as beloved children.
Help us to lay aside our envy and selfish ambition,
that we may walk in your ways of wisdom and understanding
as servants of your peace. Amen.

Jeremiah 8:18—9:1
Psalm 79:1-9
1 Timothy 2:1-7
Luke 16:1-13

When joy is gone and hearts are sick, O God,
you give us Christ as our healing balm.
He came in human flesh
that he might give himself as a ransom for our salvation
and anoint us with the Spirit of consolation and joy.
Hear the cry of your people,
that we may rejoice in the richness of your love
and be faithful stewards of your many gifts. Amen.

O God,
you call us to embrace
both you and the children of this world
with unconditional love.
Give us grace to discern
what your love demands of us,
that, being faithful in things both great and small,
we may serve you with an undivided heart. Amen.

Proper 21 [26]

Sunday between September 25 and October 1 inclusive

Thematic

See the prayers for series 1 on pp. 130–135.

Intercessory

See the seasonal options on pp. 136–138.

Scripture

YEAR A, Series 1
Exodus 17:1-7
Psalm 78:1-4, 12-16
Philippians 2:1-13
Matthew 21:23-32

Welcoming God,
you receive and bless all
who come to you in humility.
Show us our false pride,
that we may repent of all conceit and arrogance
and, caring for one another,
may honor Jesus
to the glory of your name. Amen.

YEAR A, Series 2
Ezekiel 18:1-4, 25-32
Psalm 25:1-9
Philippians 2:1-13
Matthew 21:23-32

God of our salvation,
we falter before the demands of your word
and turn away from your call to life.
Pour out your mercy on us
as you showed mercy to your people of old,
that we may turn from our sinfulness
and walk the path of self-emptying love
made known in Jesus Christ. Amen.

YEAR B, Series 1
Esther 7:1-6, 9-10; 9:20-22
Psalm 124
James 5:13-20
Mark 9:38-50

O God,
our guide and help in alien and contentious places:
as Esther prayed faithfully and worked courageously
for the deliverance of your people,
strengthen us to confront the oppressor
and free the oppressed,
so that all people may know
the justice and unity of your realm. Amen.

YEAR B, Series 2
Numbers 11:4-6, 10-16, 24-29
Psalm 19:7-14
James 5:13-20
Mark 9:38-50

Raise us up, O Lord,
for it is you alone who restores life and health
to the suffering
and to those who wander from the truth.
By your grace,
may we offer powerful and effective prayers
for one another and the world,
in the name of Jesus Christ. Amen.

YEAR C, Series 1
Jeremiah 32:1-3a, 6-15
Psalm 91:1-6, 14-16
1 Timothy 6:6-19
Luke 16:19-31

God Eternal,
you inspired Jeremiah to buy a piece of land
when no one could see a future in it.
Grant us such commitment to the future of your people,
that you will always have workers for your vineyard
and harvesters for your fields. Amen.

Holy God,
you reach out in love through Jesus Christ to save us
so that we may live as faithful servants of you alone.
Unchain us from our desire for wealth and power
so that we may, in turn, release others
from the prisons of poverty, hunger, and oppression. Amen.

Proper 22 [27]

Sunday between October 2 and 8 inclusive

Thematic

See the prayers for series 1 on pp. 130–135.

Intercessory

See the seasonal options on pp. 136–138.

Scripture

YEAR A, Series 1
Exodus 20:1-4, 7-9, 12-20
Psalm 19
Philippians 3:4b-14
Matthew 21:33-46

God, our beloved,
you set before us the goal of new life in Christ.
May we live in the power of his resurrection
and bring forth the fruit of your gentle and loving rule. Amen.

YEAR A, Series 2
Isaiah 5:1-7
Psalm 80:7-15
Philippians 3:4b-14
Matthew 21:33-46

Holy God,
you love justice and hate oppression;
you call us to righteousness and not to exploitation.
Give us generous and loving hearts,
and eyes to see the splendor of your reign,
that we may live in truth and honor,
and praise you for the transformation of our lives,
through Jesus Christ our Lord. Amen.

YEAR B, Series 1
Job 1:1; 2:1-10
Psalm 26
Hebrews 1:1-4; 2:5-12
Mark 10:2-16

Mighty and powerful God,
through Jesus Christ our Savior
you come to save people in all times and places,
offering them new life in your presence.
Give us open hearts to receive your Chosen One,
that through him we may dwell with you
as faithful and committed disciples. Amen.

YEAR B, Series 2
Genesis 2:18-24
Psalm 8
Hebrews 1:1-4; 2:5-12
Mark 10:2-16

Sovereign God,
you make us for each other,
to live in loving community
as friends, sons and daughters,
sisters and brothers, wives and husbands,
partners and companions.
Teach us to choose love
that is committed and devoted;
teach us like little children
to wonder and to trust,
that our loving may reflect the image of Christ. Amen.

YEAR C, Series 1
Lamentations 1:1-6
Lamentations 3:19-26 or Psalm 137
2 Timothy 1:1-14
Luke 17:5-10

God, the refuge of wanderers and exiles,
the mother and father of the homeless,
you weep with those who are uprooted from their homeland,
and you suffer with those who exist without shelter and security.
Grant that your faithful love may reach out,
and that your healing mercy rise like the dawn
on all who are oppressed.
We ask this through Jesus, your Son,
who knew hardship and died outside the city wall. Amen.

God of all the ages,
you have revealed your grace
in our Savior, Jesus Christ.
As we wait patiently on your mercies,
strengthen us to live in your justice,
that with open hearts we may hear
and accomplish your will,
through Christ, who lights the way to life everlasting. Amen.

Proper 23 [28]

Sunday between October 9 and 15 inclusive

Thematic

See the prayers for series 1 on pp. 130–135.

Intercessory

See the seasonal options on pp. 136–138.

Scripture

YEAR A, Series 1
Exodus 32:1-14
Psalm 106:1-6, 19-23
Philippians 4:1-9
Matthew 22:1-14

God of Aaron, Miriam, and Moses,
you stayed the hand of your wrath
when we fell into idolatry and discord;
and when we forgot our deliverance,
your love for us remained unchanging.
Transform us and our world
into a place of justice, love, and peace.
Welcome us to your wedding feast
where all are invited to be gathered in. Amen.

YEAR A, Series 2
Isaiah 25:1-9
Psalm 23
Philippians 4:1-9
Matthew 22:1-14

Lord of the feast,
you have prepared a table before all peoples
and poured out life with such abundance
that death cannot claim the triumph over your universe.
Call us again to your banquet
where we may receive your holy food,
and, strengthened by what is honorable, just, and pure,
be transformed into a people of righteousness and peace. Amen.

God, you promise never to forsake us,
but to bring us to life,
nurture us with your presence,
and sustain us even in the hour of our death.
Meet us in our deepest doubts
when we feel abandoned,
drowning in our fear of your absence.
Visit us in the tension between our yearning and our anger,
that we may know your mercy and grace in our time of need. Amen.

YEAR B, Series 2
Amos 5:6-7, 10-15
Psalm 90:12-17
Hebrews 4:12-16
Mark 10:17-31

God of all who are cast down,
you call us to seek good
and to meet oppression with justice.
Teach us to find salvation
in the emptying of ourselves for the sake of those in need,
so that goodness may prevail
and your kingdom come in Jesus Christ. Amen.

YEAR C, Series 1
Jeremiah 29:1, 4-7
Psalm 66:1-12
2 Timothy 2:8-15
Luke 17:11-19

Wholeness of the sick and Home of the exile,
give us grace to seek the well-being
of those among whom we live,
so that all people may come to know
the healing of your love
and new voices join to give you thanks in Jesus Christ. Amen.

OR

In your love, O God of hosts,
your people find healing.
Grant that the pains of our journey may not obscure
the presence of Christ among us,
but that we may always give thanks for your healing power
as we travel on the way to your kingdom.
We ask this through Jesus Christ our Lord. Amen.

YEAR C, Series 2
2 Kings 5:1-3, 7-15c
Psalm 111
2 Timothy 2:8-15
Luke 17:11-19

O God of compassion,
through the witness of a captive maidservant
you healed Naaman in the waters of the Jordan.
Through Jesus you healed the lepers.
Heal us so that we may follow Christ with joy,
giving thanks with all our being. Amen.

Proper 24 [29]

Sunday between October 16 and 22 inclusive

Thematic

See the prayers for series 1 on pp. 130–135.

Intercessory

See the seasonal options on pp. 136–138.

Scripture

YEAR A, Series 1
Exodus 33:12-23
Psalm 99
1 Thessalonians 1:1-10
Matthew 22:15-22

You know each of us by name, O God,
and in your sight we have found favor,
yet our minds cannot comprehend the vision of your glory
or the vastness of your love.
Grant that as we glimpse your greatness,
reflected in your many gifts,
we may always return to you
the praise that is yours alone.
We ask this through Jesus Christ our Lord. Amen.

YEAR A, Series 2
Isaiah 45:1-7
Psalm 96:1-9, [10-13]
1 Thessalonians 1:1-10
Matthew 22:15-22

Creator of all,
you have called us and chosen us to be your people.
By the power of your Holy Spirit
may we bear witness with joy and conviction
to the good news of Jesus Christ. Amen.

YEAR B, Series 1

Job 38:1-7, [34-41]
Psalm 104:1-9, 24, 35b
Hebrews 5:1-10
Mark 10:35-45

Creator God,
you are wrapped in light as a garment,
clothed with honor and majesty.
Enlighten us with true faith and humble obedience
that seeks to serve others in your name. Amen.

YEAR B, Series 2

Isaiah 53:4-12
Psalm 91:9-16
Hebrews 5:1-10
Mark 10:35-45

Most High,
your Anointed One offered himself freely
as witness against our violence,
our acts of oppression,
and our sin.
As you delighted to call him your Son,
give us the courage to bring you equal delight
by our willingness to drink the cup of sacrifice
on behalf of our sisters and brothers,
and, with them, offer you praise unceasing
and lives transformed
as true heirs of your grace-filled realm. Amen.

YEAR C, Series 1

Jeremiah 31:27-34
Psalm 119:97-104
2 Timothy 3:14—4:5
Luke 18:1-8

O God, Spirit of righteousness,
you temper judgment with mercy.
Help us to live the covenant written upon our hearts
so that when Christ returns
we may be found worthy
to be received into your by grace presence. Amen.

Holy One,
we lift our eyes to you in hope and awe.
Grant that we may reject all apathy of spirit,
all impatience and anxiety,
so that, with the persistence of the widow,
we may lift our voice again and again to seek your justice. Amen.

Proper 25 [30]

Sunday between October 23 and 29 inclusive

Thematic

See the prayers for series 1 on pp. 130–135.

Intercessory

See the seasonal options on pp. 136–138.

Scripture

YEAR A, Series 1
Deuteronomy 34:1-12
Psalm 90:1-6, 13-17
1 Thessalonians 2:1-8
Matthew 22:34-46

Almighty God,
your Son has shown us how to love one another.
May our love for you
overflow into joyous service
and be a healing witness to our neighbors
through Jesus Christ our Lord. Amen.

YEAR A, Series 2
Leviticus 19:1-2, 15-18
Psalm 1
1 Thessalonians 2:1-8
Matthew 22:34-46

Holy One,
you planted us by living water,
that we might be rooted in righteousness.
You call us to be holy as you are holy.
Assured of your love,
help us to cast aside all fear,
that we may love our neighbors as ourselves. Amen.

Almighty God,
creator of heaven and earth
in whom all things are possible,
have mercy on us and heal us,
that sustained by the power of your word
and by the constant intercession of our Lord and Savior,
we may draw near to you
and follow in your way as faithful disciples. Amen.

O Jesus Christ, teacher and healer,
you heard the cry of the blind beggar
when others would have silenced him.
Teach us to be persistent in prayer
and give us courage to ask plainly
what we need from you,
that we might respond in your name
by the power of the Spirit
through the ministry entrusted to us
for the sake of the gospel. Amen.

OR

O Jesus Christ, teacher and healer,
you heard the cry of the blind beggar
when others would have silenced him.
Teach us to be attentive
to the voices others ignore,
that we might respond
through the power of the Spirit
to heal the afflicted
and to welcome the abandoned
for your sake and the sake of the gospel. Amen.

YEAR C, Series 1
Joel 2:23-32
Psalm 65
2 Timothy 4:6-8, 16-18
Luke 18:9-14

O Wellspring of salvation,
we come to you in joy,
for you have heard the prayers of the poor
and raised up the lowly.
Pour out your Spirit
on young and old alike,
that our dreams and visions may bring
justice and peace to the world. Amen.

YEAR C, Series 2
Sirach 35:12-17 or Jeremiah 14:7-10, 19-22
Psalm 84:1-7
2 Timothy 4:6-8, 16-18
Luke 18:9-14

O God,
the strength of those who humbly confess their sin
and place their hope in you,
save us from vain displays of righteousness,
and give us grace to keep faith
with the true humility of our Lord Jesus Christ. Amen.

Proper 26 [31]

Sunday between October 30 and November 5 inclusive

Thematic

See the prayers for series 1 on pp. 130–135.

Intercessory

See the seasonal options on pp. 136–138.

Scripture

YEAR A, Series 1
Joshua 3:7-17
Psalm 107:1-7, 33-37
1 Thessalonians 2:9-13
Matthew 23:1-12

Your steadfast love endures from age to age, O living God,
for in Christ you tenderly care for your people.
Instruct us in your way of humble service,
that we may imitate his saving deeds
who humbled himself for our salvation
and is now exalted with you in splendor
for ever and ever. Amen.

YEAR A, Series 2
Micah 3:5-12
Psalm 43
1 Thessalonians 2:9-13
Matthew 23:1-12

O God, your Spirit speaks through your prophets,
protecting your people
from those who would lead them astray.
Raise up new voices in our time
to speak with justice and power
and to challenge the complacency
that would have us rest easily with sin. Amen.

Beloved Companion,
you deal with us kindly in steadfast love,
lifting up those bent low with care
and sustaining the weak and oppressed.
Release us from our anxious fears,
that we, holding fast to your commandments,
may honor you with all that we are
and all that we have. Amen.

Eternal God,
teach us to love you not only in mind and heart
but also in purpose and action,
that we may love the children of the earth,
in Jesus Christ. Amen.

In your Son you seek out and save the lost, O God,
and invite us to the banquet of your eternal home.
Visit your people with the joy of salvation,
that we may rejoice in the riches of your forgiveness
and reach out in welcome to share with others
the feast of your love. Amen.

Holy God,
all our worship is met by the cleansing gaze of your passion for justice.
Enfold us in your grace
that we may embody our devotion in acts of justice
and in defense of the helpless,
to the glory of your name. Amen.

Proper 27 [32]

Sunday between November 6 and 12 inclusive

Thematic

See the prayers for series 1 on pp. 130–135.

Intercessory

God of life, we praise you for your abiding presence
from generation to generation,
blessing your people,
strengthening us to lives of service,
empowering us to witness.
Hear the prayers we offer on behalf of your creation.

Prayers of the People, concluding with:

Grant that as we serve you now on earth,
so we may one day rejoice with all the saints
in your kingdom of light and peace,
through Jesus Christ our Lord. Amen.

Scripture

YEAR A, Series 1
Joshua 24:1-3a, 14-25
Psalm 78:1-7
1 Thessalonians 4:13-18
Matthew 25:1-13

You let us choose, O God,
between you and the false gods of this world.
In the midst of the night of sin and death,
wake us from our slumber
and call us forth to greet Christ,
so that with eyes and hearts fixed on him,
we may follow to eternal light. Amen.

YEAR A, Series 2
Wisdom of Solomon 6:12-16 *or* Amos 5:18-24
Wisdom of Solomon 6:17-20 *or* Psalm 70
1 Thessalonians 4:13-18
Matthew 25:1-13

Ever-living God,
you inscribe our names in your book of life
so that we may share in the firstfruits of salvation.
Grant that we may acknowledge Christ as our redeemer
and, trusting in him,
be confident that none of your own will be lost or forgotten.
We ask this in the name of Jesus the Lord. Amen.

YEAR B, Series 1
Ruth 3:1-5; 4:13-17
Psalm 127
Hebrews 9:24-28
Mark 12:38-44

God our redeemer,
in sustaining the lives of Naomi and Ruth,
you gave new life to your people.
We ask that from age to age,
new generations may be born
to restore life and nourish the weak,
by returning to you
those things we once thought ours. Amen.

YEAR B, Series 2
1 Kings 17:8-16
Psalm 146
Hebrews 9:24-28
Mark 12:38-44

God of widows and strangers,
you protect the oppressed and forgotten
and feed the hungry with good things.
You stand among us in Christ, offering life to all.
Give us open hearts and minds
to respond with love to the world,
caring for those for whom you care. Amen.

Almighty God,
you hold all the powers of the universe within your hands,
and we are your children.
Turn us to the splendor of life in you,
transforming us through Jesus Christ our Savior,
and strengthening us in every good deed and word. Amen.

Eternally righteous God,
merciful judge of all the living:
in your love you called us
to share the glory of Christ.
Strengthen our hearts in every good work and word,
that we may be steadfast in your ways
and always believe your truth. Amen.

Proper 28 [33]

Sunday between November 13 and 19 inclusive

Thematic

See the prayers for series 1 on pp. 130–135.

Intercessory

See the seasonal options on pp. 136–138.

Scripture

YEAR A, Series 1
Judges 4:1-7
Psalm 123
1 Thessalonians 5:1-11
Matthew 25:14-30

God of the covenant,
even when we fall into sin,
your Spirit invites us to remember
that you chose us to be your servant people.
Awaken us to the power and gifts
you pour into us for the good of creation,
and grant that we may be trustworthy in all things,
producing abundantly as we work to build your realm. Amen.

YEAR A, Series 2
Zephaniah 1:7, 12-18
Psalm 90:1-8, [9-11], 12
1 Thessalonians 5:1-11
Matthew 25:14-30

You, O God, are our dwelling-place
from generation to generation,
our shield from anguish and distress.
You arm us as children of light
with the hope of salvation,
and you protect us by your love.
Give us grace to build up
and encourage one another,
as we seek wisdom and abundant life
in the strength of your Word
and the assurance of your Spirit. Amen.

God our rock,
you hear the cries of your people
and answer the prayers of the faithful.
Grant us the boldness of Hannah
that we may persist in prayer,
confident in your steadfast love. Amen.

Timeless One,
you create all moments of our lives,
giving each its meaning and purpose.
Strengthen us to witness continually
to the love of Jesus Christ,
that we may hold fast in times of trial,
even to the end of the ages. Amen.

O God,
in Christ you give us hope
for a new heaven and a new earth.
Grant us wisdom to interpret the signs of our times,
courage to stand in the time of trial,
and faith to witness to your truth and love. Amen.

God, our God,
you hear our cry and listen to our prayer.
Grant that we may know that our redeemer lives
and, trusting in you,
be confident that we will not be lost or forgotten.
We ask this in the name of Jesus the Lord. Amen.

Proper 29 [34]

Reign of Christ or *Christ the King*
Sunday between November 20 and 26 inclusive

Thematic

Shepherd of Israel, hear our prayer
as your Son heard the plea
of the criminal crucified with him.
Gather into Christ's holy reign
the broken, the sorrowing, and the sinner,
that all may know
wholeness, joy, and forgiveness. Amen.

Intercessory

As the shepherd who cares for the flock, O God,
you guide all things through Jesus
whom you have exalted over all creation as king.
Hear the prayers we offer in his name
for the creation he cherished
and that you entrust to us.

Prayers of the People, concluding with:

Look upon your people who rejoice in your justice and mercy,
and grant that the prayers we make
may reveal Christ's reign in our time. Amen.

Scripture

YEAR A, Series 1
Ezekiel 34:11-16, 20-24
Psalm 100
Ephesians 1:15-23
Matthew 25:31-46

You raised up your Son, O God,
and seated him at your right hand
as the shepherd and king
who seeks what is lost,
binds up what is wounded,
and strengthens what is weak.
Empowered by the Spirit,
grant that we may share with others
that which we have received from your hand,
to the honor of Jesus Christ our Lord. Amen.

OR

Lord God,
your power was revealed
when you raised Christ from the dead
and seated him at your right hand.
Grant that we may always give you thanks
for your immeasurable love
and show that gratitude in loving service
to all our brothers and sisters
through Jesus Christ. Amen.

YEAR A, Series 2
Ezekiel 34:11-16, 20-24
Psalm 95:1-7a
Ephesians 1:15-23
Matthew 25:31-46

O God,
in Jesus Christ we celebrate your power at work.
You raised him from the dead
to rule with you forevermore.
Enlighten the eyes of our hearts,
that we may see the hope
to which Christ calls us,
a realm of eternal peace. Amen.

YEAR B, Series 1
2 Samuel 23:1-7
Psalm 132:1-12, [13-18]
Revelation 1:4b-8
John 18:33-37

Almighty God,
you remembered the oath you swore to David
and so established a glorious realm of salvation
through Jesus of Nazareth, his heir.
Train our eyes to see your righteous rule,
that, standing firmly in hope
before the powers of this world,
we may heed your voice
and be constant in your truth. Amen.

Most High God, majestic and almighty,
our beginning and our end:
rule in our hearts
and guide us to be faithful in our daily actions,
worshiping the one who comes
as Savior and Sovereign,
and who lives and reigns with you
in the unity of the Holy Spirit, one God. Amen.

Almighty God,
you rescue us from our enemies,
that we may serve you without fear.
Strengthen us,
that we may share in the inheritance of the saints
in your kingdom of light. Amen.

Holy God, our refuge and strength,
you have redeemed your scattered children,
gathering them from all the corners of the earth
through your firstborn, the Christ,
in whom all things are held together.
Make of us a just and righteous people,
worthy by grace to inherit with him
the kingdom of light and peace
where he reigns with you and the Holy Spirit. Amen.

Special Days

Presentation of the Lord
February 2

Thematic

God of steadfast love,
you sent your Son to be the light of the world,
saving people everywhere from sin and death.
As Anna gave thanks for the freedom he would bring,
and Simeon saw in him the dawn of redemption,
complete your purpose once made known in him.
Make us the vessels of his light,
that all the world may glory in the splendor of your peace. Amen.

Intercessory

God of love,
you refine silver and shelter the sparrow's nest.
Accept the prayers we bring this day,
for you know all that tests and troubles us.

Prayers of the People, concluding with:

Embrace our needs in your blessing,
so that we may be sustained,
even in times of trial. Amen.

Scripture

YEAR A, B, C
Malachi 3:1-4
Psalm 84 *or* Psalm 24:7-10
Hebrews 2:14-18
Luke 2:22-40

Strong and mighty God, Father of our Lord Jesus,
the presentation of your Son in the temple
was his first entrance into the place of sacrifice.
Grant that, trusting in his offering upon the cross
to forgive our sins and uphold us in the time of trial,
we may sing your praises
and live in the light of your salvation, Jesus Christ. Amen.

Annunciation of the Lord
March 25

Thematic

O God,
we rejoice in your salvation,
for your Spirit brought to life in Mary
the one who saves your people from their sins.
Send your Spirit on your church
to quicken all that is barren in us,
that we may give birth to Christ
for our world today. Amen.

Intercessory

O Loving One,
your daughter Mary prayed to be your faithful servant.
Hear the prayers of our hearts on behalf of your world.

[The Prayers of the People, concluding with:]

Ever-surprising One,
as your messenger came to Mary
with words of your favor
and the pledge of wondrous new life,
may we, in our day,
prove ourselves
as ready to serve you,
and as willing to bear the life you offer,
for the blessing of our world. Amen.

Scripture

YEAR A, B, C
Isaiah 7:10-14
Psalm 45 *or* Psalm 40:5-10
Hebrews 10:4-10
Luke 1:26-38

God of impossibilities,
you chose to enter human flesh
through the one who called herself lowly.
Teach us who daily receive announcements of Christ's coming
to live as Mary did,
trusting in your power
to bring your desire to fulfillment. Amen.

Visitation of Mary to Elizabeth

May 31

Thematic

Blessed God,
who danced in our hearts,
filling us with the knowledge of your presence:
let your proclamation sing forth from us
as it sang from the lips of Hannah and Elizabeth,
announcing the coming of your promise
and the fulfillment of your desire. Amen.

Intercessory

Blessed are you, God of glory and majesty,
for you announced the coming of your Son,
who brings joy and gladness to this waiting world.
Receive our prayers offered in the confidence
that you are present,
working to answer the needs of your people.

Prayers of the People, concluding with:

Grant that we may hasten to every town and home
with the good news of your promise, O God,
and proclaim the greatness of your name
through our commitment to your peace. Amen.

Scripture

YEAR A, B, C
1 Samuel 2:1-10
Psalm 113
Romans 12:9-16b
Luke 1:39-57

Blessed God,
who invited us to be handmaids of your creative power:
Bless us as you blessed Hannah, Elizabeth, and Mary,
filling our barren hearts with your fertile word,
nurturing faith within us,
sustaining us as we ripen with hope,
until your desire calls us to the time of labor,
and we give birth to your incarnate love. Amen.

Holy Cross
September 14

Intercessory

In the cross our need meets God's redemption.
In confidence and hope,
we bring the prayers of our hearts
for the transformation of the church and the world.

Prayers of the People, concluding with:

Accept our prayers, God of mercy,
in union with Jesus the Christ,
who offered his life for our salvation
upon the wood of the cross
and who now reigns with you in eternal glory
forever and ever. Amen.

Scripture

YEAR A, B, C
Numbers 21:4b-9
Psalm 98:1-5 *or* Psalm 78:1-2, 34-38
1 Corinthians 1:18-24
John 3:13-17

For the healing of the nations, O God,
you raised up your Son on the wood of the cross
and exalted him as the Lord of all creation.
Grant that all who believe in him
may have the gift of eternal life
and share in the glory of your kingdom,
where you live forever and ever. Amen.

All Saints

November 1

Thematic

God of unfailing light,
in your realm of glory
the poor are blessed,
the hungry filled,
and every tear is wiped away.
Strengthened by this vision,
may we follow in the way of holiness
that your Son made known in life and death. Amen.

Intercessory

All blessing, honor, and glory,
all wisdom, praise, and thanks be yours,
O God of our salvation!
We pray in communion with all the saints on earth and heaven,
with the martyrs and the faithful in all ages,
and in the name of the Lamb who was slain,
who alone is worthy of worship.

Prayers of the People, concluding with:

Bless us with your healing presence;
make us hungry for justice;
strengthen our faith;
and increase our love for others,
especially those we find it most difficult to love. Amen.

Scripture

YEAR A
Revelation 7:9-17
Psalm 34:1-10, 22
1 John 3:1-3
Matthew 5:1-12

God of the ages,
your saints who lived in faithful service
surround your throne
and offer you praise and worship both night and day.
May we, your saints on earth,
join our voices with theirs to proclaim
your rule of righteousness and peace,
which comes to us through Jesus Christ
now and forever. Amen.

YEAR B
Wisdom of Solomon 3:1-9 *or* Isaiah 25:6-9
Psalm 24
Revelation 21:1-6a
John 11:32-44

Source of all being, beginning and end,
we praise you for those who have served you faithfully.
For the sake of Jesus Christ,
replenish our hope in your eternal kingdom,
that we may have life in all its fullness,
unfettered by the fear of death. Amen.

YEAR C
Daniel 7:1-3, 15-18
Psalm 149
Ephesians 1:11-23
Luke 6:20-31

O Ancient of Days,
through the outpouring of your Holy Spirit
you comfort and bless all creatures.
Gather from the four corners of the world
all those who weep in despair or loneliness,
those who are hungry, naked, or poor,
those who have withstood oppression
and are bowed in anguish before violence.
Grant that they may rejoice in the new life
of justice and peace that you promised your people
through the compassionate witness of Jesus. Amen.

Thanksgiving Day

October—Canada
November—USA

Thematic

O God,
in your Son Jesus Christ
you richly bless us with all that we need,
bread from the earth and the bread of heaven,
which gives life to the world.
Grant us one thing more:
grateful hearts to sing your praise,
in this world and the world to come. Amen.

Intercessory

God clothes the grass of the field
and feeds the birds of the air.
On behalf of the church and the world,
we offer our prayers
more from our need to be transformed by our awareness of them
than from any need of God to be reminded of them.

Prayers of the People, concluding with:

Free us from all fear and worry
that, trusting in your goodness,
we may always praise your mighty deeds
and give you thanks for the bounty of your gifts.
We make our prayer through Jesus Christ our Lord. Amen.

Scripture

YEAR A
Deuteronomy 8:7-18
Psalm 65
2 Corinthians 9:6-15
Luke 17:11-19

Giving and forgiving God,
you created the good earth and blessed it.
Give us glad and generous hearts,
that we may rejoice and give thanks for
the abundance of your creation,
the depths of your mercy,
and your care for all. Amen.

YEAR B
Joel 2:21-27
Psalm 126
1 Timothy 2:1-7
Matthew 6:25-33

God of the living,
with all your creatures great and small
we sing your bounty and your goodness,
for in the harvest of land and ocean,
in the cycles of the seasons,
and the wonders of each creature,
you reveal your generosity.
Teach us the gratitude that dispels envy,
that we may honor each gift as you cherish your creation,
and praise you in all times and places. Amen.

YEAR C
Deuteronomy 26:1-11
Psalm 100
Philippians 4:4-9
John 6:25-35

Generous God,
you brought us into the abundance of our inheritance.
Grant us the faith to be people
blossoming with honor and truth,
so that we may produce bountifully
the firstfruits of justice and compassion,
which are pleasing in your sight. Amen.

WRITERS OF THE PRAYERS

ANDREA LA SONDE ANASTOS was ordained to the Unitarian Universalist Christian ministry in 1985. She holds a B.F.A. in theatre from the School of Fine Arts at Boston University and an M.Div. from Harvard Divinity School. She recently completed a fourteen-year co-pastorate with her husband. She is a trained spiritual director and a trained intentional interim minister. She edited and wrote introductions for a collection of religious fantasies called *Nine Visions* and wrote *Lectionary Prayers,* a three-year cycle of collects and pastoral prayers. She also writes extensively for professional journals. Ms. Anastos has been a member of the Consultation on Common Texts (CCT) for fourteen years and served as chair of the editorial board of this project.

E. BYRON ANDERSON was ordained as an elder/presbyter in the United Methodist Church in 1986. He holds his M.Div. from Yale Divinity School and the Yale Institute of Sacred Music, and his Ph.D. is from Emory University. He is the assistant professor of worship and the director of community worship at Christian Theological Seminary in Indianapolis. Dr. Anderson's ecumenical work includes editing *The Word in Worship* for the National Council of Churches, and *Faith Alive*, an adult education program about ecumenism, for the Minnesota Council of Churches. He has also edited the two volume work, *Worship Matters,* and co-edited *Liturgy and the Moral Self.*

ALAN F. DETSCHER was ordained to the Roman Catholic priesthood in 1971. He then went on to receive a doctorate in sacred liturgy *summa cum laude* from the Pontifical Liturgical Institute in Rome in 1981. He is currently the director of the office of ecumenical affairs of the Diocese of Bridgeport and an associate pastor of St. Catherine of Siena parish in Riverside, Connecticut. Monsignor Detscher has served for thirty years on the International Commission on English in the Liturgy and was the director of the secretariat of the Bishops' Committee on Liturgy. He is a member of Societas Liturgica and the North American Academy of Liturgy and is the current chair of the CCT. He served as a member of the editorial board of this project.

PAUL FAYTER began his pastoral ministry in 1984, received an M.Div. in 1991, and was ordained in The United Church of Canada in 1992. He also holds an M.A. in the history of science and medicine, a certificate in bioethics, and is a doctoral candidate at the University of Toronto. He is a pastor at First-Pilgrim United Church in Hamilton (Ontario) and a professor at York University in Toronto. Since 1976, he has written extensively in areas as diverse as liturgy, the history of science, science and theology, and popular culture, and made numerous television appearances in Canada. He won a 1999 Templeton Foundation award for Excellence in Teaching Science and Religion from Berkeley.

KEVIN FLYNN was ordained to the priesthood in the Anglican Church of Canada in 1983. He serves the congregation of St. Stephen-in-the-Fields in Toronto and has been lecturer in liturgics at Trinity College. He is a candidate for a D.Min. degree in the Toronto School of Theology. He is also the associate ecumenical officer of the Diocese of Toronto. Father Flynn was a member of the editorial board of this project. He is also the editor of *Let Us Keep the Feast: A Guide to the Celebration of Lent, Holy Week, and Easter.*

ANDREW FULLERTON was ordained in the Presbyterian Church in Canada in 1990 after receiving his M.Div. from Knox College in Toronto. He holds a Ph.D. from Cambridge University. He represented the Presbyterian Church in Canada at the CCT from 1994 through 1996. Currently he serves as minister of St. Andrew's Church (Stratford, Ontario) and as lecturer at Knox College.

BERNADETTE GASSLEIN is a Roman Catholic laywoman. She is the editor of *Celebrate!* magazine, a four-time winner of Catholic Church Press Association's Award for Best Editorial. *Celebrate!* also won a General Excellence Award for Specialized and Professional Magazines in 2000. She is the director of liturgy at St. Joseph's Cathedral in Edmonton (Canada) where she is also an instructor in liturgical music. She wrote the text, "O First-Born Daughter," which won the Mariological Society of North America's competition for new Marian hymns. Ms. Gasslein has written extensively in the area of liturgy and language, including "The Experience of our Language" in *La dynamique symbolique,* "Images de Marie, Images de la Femme" in *Le Supplément,* and *Preparing and Evaluating Liturgy.*

PAUL GIBSON was ordained to the priesthood in the Anglican Church of Canada in 1957. He recently retired as liturgical officer of the Anglican Church of Canada, but continues to work as coordinator for liturgy for the Anglican Consultative Commission. Dr. Gibson has served as chair of the CCT and on the sub-committee that produced the Revised Common Lectionary. His writings include *Say What You Mean,* "Worship in the Small Congregation" in *New Possibilities for Small Churches,* three volumes of short sermons, and *Patterns of Celebration: Layers of Meaning in the Structure of the Eucharist.*

FRED KIMBALL GRAHAM was baptized in The United Church of Canada and currently serves that church as officer for worship and music. He is an accomplished musician and organist, with an M.A. in music from the Eastman School. He is a recipient of a Gold Medal for Organ Performance from the Royal Conservatory in Toronto and was recently named professor of church music at Emmanuel College. He has a Ph.D. in liturgical theology from Drew University. His ecumenical projects include 13 years with the CCT and and 12 years of work with the Canadian Council of Churches. He was assistant editor of the hymnal *Voices United* and supervising editor of *Celebrate God's Presence* (a book of services).

JUDEE ARCHER GREEN was ordained in the Presbyterian Church in Canada in 1977. She holds a B.Math. from the University of Waterloo in mathematics and computer science and her M.Div. from Knox College in Toronto. In addition to being a member of the CCT and the editorial board of this project, her ecumenical work includes the book *Holy Time: Seven Seasons of Jubilee.* Currently she is chaplain at Crieff Hills Community Retreat Centre outside Toronto, and clerk of the presbytery of Hamilton. She was co-editor of the Presbyterian worship resource, *The Book of Psalms,* and served on the Presbyterian Church in Canada's task force for the 1997 revision of *The Book of Praise.*

CLIFTON F. GUTHRIE is an Episcopal layman with a Ph.D. from Emory University. He is assistant professor of homiletics and pastoral studies at Bangor (Maine) Theological Seminary, a seminary affiliated with The United Church of Christ. He is the editor of *Doxology: A Journal of Worship* and *For All the Saints: A Calendar of Commemorations for United Methodists.* His research interests include lay preaching and the dialogue between science and religion.

JOHN HIBBARD was born and raised in the eastern townships of Quebec. His graduate studies in theology were completed at St. Augustine's Seminary in Toronto and he holds a master's degree in liturgical studies from the University of Notre Dame (Indiana). He was ordained to the priesthood of the Roman Catholic Church in 1974 and has served primarily as a parish priest since that time. He is currently the pastor at St. John Bosco Parish in Brockville, Ontario, and master of ceremonies for the archdiocese of Kingston. In 1990, he was appointed director of the National Liturgical Office of the Canadian Conference of Catholic Bishops, during which time he served as a member of the CCT. Father Hibbard continues to lecture and give workshops on liturgy.

DEBORAH O'NEAL LANNON was ordained in the Presbyterian Church in Canada in 1988. She has completed two congregational ministries: one in Toronto and one in Regina. She served as a member of the task force that developed *The Book of Psalms,* a congregational worship resource for singing and reading the psalms.

ANDRE LAVERGNE was ordained in the Evangelical Lutheran Church in Canada (ELCIC) in 1980 and currently serves with the community of Trinity Lutheran Church in New Hamburg, Ontario. He has served on both the synodical and national worship committees of the ELCIC and as the ELCIC's national staff person for worship. He has lectured at Waterloo Lutheran Seminary. Ecumenically, he has been a delegate to the CCT. With the Rev. Wendell Grahlman, he maintains the internationally-acclaimed spirituality and worship website, *Lift Up Your Hearts* (www.worship.ca).

Barbara Liotscos was ordained a priest in the Anglican Church of Canada in 1981 after receiving her M.Div. from Vancouver School of Theology. She also holds a Th.M. from Trinity College in Toronto. She is a past member of the CCT and the recent national consultant for ministry and worship of the Anglican Church of Canada. Her ecumenical writings include *Holy Time: Seven Seasons of Jubilee* and *Gathered in Christ* (resource materials for the Week of Prayer for Christian Unity.) She has also published a number of articles in the area of liturgy and worship. Currently she is serving as in the diocese of Kootenay.

Louise Mangan received her M.Div. from the Vancouver School of Theology and Emmanuel College in Toronto before being ordained in The United Church of Canada in 1992. Currently she serves as the pastoral minister of Oakridge United Church in Vancouver. She was led to ordained ministry through her work as founding chair of the Midwifery Task Force of British Columbia that launched the rebirth of midwifery across Canada. With Lori Farr and Nancy Wyse, she is the co-author of *Living the Christ-Life: Rediscovering the Christian Year*. Ms. Mangan has served on two national committees for The United Church of Canada.

Arlene Martin Mark is a laywoman in the Mennonite Church. Her graduate studies took place at the University of Notre Dame and the Associated Mennonite Biblical Seminary. Her writings include *Worship Resources* and *Words for Worship*. Ms. Mark is a committed volunteer, currently serving as vice chair of the board for Church Community Services, an ecumenical agency helping the poor. She was the first woman in her congregation to preach, to be elected to the council, and to serve as moderator of council. She was also the first woman to be elected chair of the Goshen College (Indiana) Board of Overseers.

Blair Gilmer Meeks is a United Methodist laywoman active in the drama, worship, and teaching ministries of her church. She is the former editor of the journal, *Liturgy*. As a writer, her articles, prayers and sermons are widely published in a number of books and journals. She also compiled and edited the book, *Landscape of Praise,* which won the Catholic Press Association Award for Liturgy.

Clayton L. Morris was a member of the editorial board of this project. He was ordained to the priesthood in the Episcopal Church (U.S.A.) in 1972 and received his Ph.D. in theology from the Graduate Theological Union in 1986. He is currently the liturgical officer for the Episcopal Church. His writings in the area of liturgy include *Prayer Book Revision or Liturgical Renewal?*, *Incarnation into Culture: Becoming a Church in a New Millenium.* He is also editor of *As We Gather to Pray: An Episcopal Guide to Worship.*

MARY KATHLEEN SPEEGLE SCHMITT was ordained to the priesthood in the Anglican Church of Canada in 1984 and has served three pastorates in the diocese of Edmonton and New Westminster (Canada). She has also served on the liturgical sub-committee of the Faith, Worship and Ministry Committee of the Anglican Church of Canada. She is currently working with her husband, Ed, in the diocese of El Salvador where she serves as a pastor and educator. Her writings include *Seasons of the Feminine Divine: Christian Feminist Prayers for the Liturgical Cycle* and the winning short story of 1998 in *Amethyst Review*. She has been active for many years in ecumenical projects including "Ten Days for World Development."

DIANE J. STRICKLAND was ordained in the Presbyterian Church in Canada in 1988 after receiving her M.Div. from Knox College in the Toronto School of Theology. Ms. Strickland is a past member of the CCT and served as worship officer of the Presbyterian Church in Canada from 1992 to 1995. She was co-editor of the Presbyterian worship resource, *The Book of Psalms*, and her sermons are published in two collections of sermons by women, *Brave Souls on a Terrible Day* and *The Woman with the Flow of Blood*. She recently completed a co-ministry with her husband in Manitoba. In addition to her pastoral work, Ms. Strickland designs liturgical art and vestments.

MAREN TIRABASSI holds her M.Div. from Union Seminary (NY) and a Th.M. from Harvard Divinity School. She was ordained in the United Church of Christ in 1981. She is a poet, liturgical writer, and currently serves as pastor of Northwood Congregational Church in New Hampshire. She teaches poetry in schools and prisons and leads retreats and seminars to help clergy and laity shape worship. Her latest book of poetry is *The Depth of Wells*. Other books include *Faith Made Visible* (with Charles McCollugh), *Gifts of Many Cultures* (with Kathy Wonson Eddy), and *Touch Holiness* (with Ruth C. Duck).

NIGEL ALASTAIR MCKAY WEAVER was ordained in The United Church of Canada in 1991. He was born in London, England. His writings and hymns, including "The Risen Christ," have appeared in various United Church of Canada publications. Another hymn, "We Sing the Three Who Are One," debuted in the Celtic worship at the Renovations 2000 conference. He has served both rural and urban congregations and is trained in intentional interim ministry. At present, he is serving with the congregation of Manor Road United Church in Toronto.

INDEX

Scripture Readings in Biblical Order

Two symbols are used to indicate the two distinct patterns of Old Testament readings (and psalms) on the Sundays that follow Pentecost (Proper 4 through Proper 29). The symbol (†) indicates the pattern of semicontinuous Old Testament readings. The symbol (*) indicates the pattern of paired readings in which the Old Testament reading and the gospel reading are closely related. Since each pattern has its own consistency, it is important to select one or the other for use throughout the Sundays that follow Pentecost in a particular year.

"Alt" indicates an alternate reading or response appointed for the day. "Resp" indicates a response (to the first reading) that is not from the psalms.

Gn 1:1—2:4a	Trinity Sunday	A		Gn 45:1-15†	Proper 15 [20]	A
Gn 1:1—2:4a	Easter Vigil	ABC		Gn 45:3-11, 15	Epiphany 7 [7]	C
Gn 1:1-5	Baptism of the Lord [1]	B		Gn 50:15-21*	Proper 19 [24]	A
Gn 2:15-17; 3:1-7	Lent 1	A				
				Ex 1:8—2:10†	Proper 16 [21]	A
Gn 2:18-24*	Proper 22 [27]	B		Ex 3:1-15†	Proper 17 [22]	A
Gn 3:8-15*	Proper 5 [10]	B		Ex 12:1-14†	Proper 18 [23]	A
Gn 6:9-22; 7:24; 8:14-19†	Proper 4 [9]	A		Ex 12:1-4, [5-10], 11-14	Holy Thursday	ABC
Gn 7:1-5, 11-18; 8:6-18; 9:8-13	Easter Vigil	ABC		Ex 14:10-31; 15:20-21	Easter Vigil	ABC
Gn 9:8-17	Lent 1	B		Ex 14:19-31†	Proper 19 [24]	A
Gn 11:1-9 (Alt)	Pentecost	C		Ex 15:1b-11, 20-21 (Alt resp)†	Proper 19 [24]	A
Gn 12:1-4a	Lent 2	A				
Gn 12:1-9†	Proper 5 [10]	A		Ex 15:1b-13, 17-18 (resp)	Easter Vigil	ABC
Gn 15:1-6*	Proper 14 [19]	C				
Gn 15:1-12, 17-18	Lent 2	C		Ex 16:2-4, 9-15*	Proper 13 [18]	B
				Ex 16:2-15†	Proper 20 [25]	A
Gn 17:1-7, 15-16	Lent 2	B		Ex 17:1-7	Lent 3	A
Gn 18:1-15, [21:1-17]†	Proper 6 [11]	A		Ex 17:1-7†	Proper 21 [26]	A
				Ex 19:2-8a*	Proper 6 [11]	A
Gn 18:1-10a*	Proper 11 [16]	C		Ex 20:1-4, 7-9, 12-20†	Proper 22 [27]	A
Gn 18:20-32*	Proper 12 [17]	C				
Gn 21:8-21†	Proper 7 [12]	A		Ex 20:1-17	Lent 3	B
Gn 22:1-14†	Proper 8 [13]	A		Ex 24:12-18	Epiphany Last Transfig.	A
Gn 22:1-18	Easter Vigil	ABC		Ex 32:1-14†	Proper 23 [28]	A
Gn 24:34-38, 42-49, 58-67†	Proper 9 [14]	A		Ex 32:7-14*	Proper 19 [24]	C
				Ex 33:12-23†	Proper 24 [29]	A
Gn 25:19-34†	Proper 10 [15]	A		Ex 34:29-35	Epiphany Last Transfig.	C
Gn 28:10-19a†	Proper 11 [16]	A				
Gn 29:15-28†	Proper 12 [17]	A		Lv 19:1-2, 9-18	Epiphany 7 [7]	A
Gn 32:22-31†	Proper 13 [18]	A		Lv 19:1-2, 15-18*	Proper 25 [30]	A
Gn 32:22-31*	Proper 24 [29]	C				
Gn 37:1-4, 12-28†	Proper 14 [19]	A		Nm 6:22-27	Holy Name	ABC

Questionnaire

This questionnaire is for use by congregations and individuals who desire to participate in the evaluation of these prayers. In the case of evaluations by congregations or groups, it would be especially helpful if a single questionnaire representing the evaluation of the whole group could be prepared. Feedback received will help to shape the subsequent revision of this material. Please feel free to continue your responses on additional pages as necessary.

Information about this evaluation

Name of individual or group

Position or Title

Congregation, Organization, or Community

Denomination

Address

E-mail address

If this is an individual response, please answer the following:

I am: _____ Female _____ Male
I am: _____ Lay _____ Clergy _____ Other (e. g., Spiritual Director)
I am: _____ Staff _____ Non-staff

If you feel your ethnic background is applicable to your responses, would you indicate what that background is? _____

If you feel your denominational background is applicable to your response, would you indicate what that background is? _____

My role or function in public worship (check all that apply)

_____ presiding _____ preaching
_____ reading scripture _____ leading prayer
_____ leading or making music _____ worshiping in the assembly
_____ other:

How did you use the content of this resource?

Did you:

study the contents of this resource privately?	YES	NO
study the contents with a small group?	YES	NO
use the contents for personal devotions?	YES	NO
study the contents with an ecumenical group?	YES	NO

Other:

Comments:

Setting of the evaluation

If these prayers were evaluated through their use in corporate worship, in what kind of setting did this take place?

_____ parish or congregation   _____ religious community

_____ retreat house   _____ seminary or theological school

_____ campus ministry (college/university)

_____ other:

Comments:

Over what period were the prayers used?

_____ three years or more

_____ two–three years

_____ one–two years

_____ less than a year

Comments:

Use of the prayers and the Revised Common Lectionary (RCL)

Which of the types of prayers did you use? (check all that apply)

_____   Thematic Prayers

_____   Intercessory Prayers

_____   Scripture Prayers

How do you use these prayers in worship?

What is your usual experience of the use of the RCL readings?

_____   every Sunday

_____   most Sundays

_____   occasionally

_____   We use a different lectionary than RCL. (Which? _____)

_____   other:

What is the usual experience of preaching on the lectionary in your community?

_____   every Sunday

_____   most Sundays

_____   occasionally

_____   other:

Evaluation of Prayers

General comments about the resource:

Have these prayers broadened and recovered the use of biblical imagery?
This strategy is:

Successful   Unsuccessful
1   2   3   4   5

Comments:

Have the prayers acknowledged the tension between the Old and New Testaments?
This strategy is:

Successful   Unsuccessful
1   2   3   4   5

Comments:

Do the prayers reflect a balance of liturgical year orientation and scriptural focus?
This strategy is:

Successful   Unsuccessful
1   2   3   4   5

Comments:

Are the prayers sufficiently succinct and concise, avoiding filler words and phrases?
This strategy is:

Successful   Unsuccessful
1   2   3   4   5

Comments:

Do these prayers avoid theological jargon without being devoid of theological content?
This strategy is:

Successful   Unsuccessful
1   2   3   4   5

Comments:

Do the prayers reflect issues and concerns of the marginalized and disenfranchised?
This strategy is:

Successful   Unsuccessful
1   2   3   4   5

Comments:

Do these prayers reflect a breadth of imagery, language, style, and experience?
This strategy is:

Successful   Unsuccessful

1   2   3   4   5

Comments:

Is this collection of prayers useful and fitting for public and corporate worship?
It is:

Useful and fitting   Not useful or fitting

1   2   3   4   5

Comments:

What has been the response to the startling or unexpected scriptural and poetic images used in some of these prayers?

What are the strengths of these prayers based on the Revised Common Lectionary?

What are the weaknesses of these prayers based on the Revised Common Lectionary?

Are the above principles that underline the composition of these prayers adequate to the needs of your community?

Comments or suggestions for revisions of specific prayers. *(Please be specific in your comments and refer to the page and number of each prayer. For example, the third prayer on page 130 may be indicated by 130:3.)*

Is there anything else you want to tell us that we haven't asked?

Completed questionnaires may be sent directly to the secretariat of the CCT:
Consultation on Common Texts
c/o The Rev. Daniel Benedict
P. O. Box 340003
Nashville, TN 37203-0003
www.commontexts.org